T0364176

THE BOOK OF DANGEROUS WORDS IN MANAGEMENT

The original edition was published
in 2017 by Campus Verlag with the title
Gefährliche Managementwörter.

Fredmund Malik

THE BOOK OF DANGEROUS WORDS IN MANAGEMENT

Translated from German
by Joe Kroll

Campus Verlag
Frankfurt/New York

ISBN 978-3-593-51160-3 Print
ISBN 978-3-593-44327-0 E-Book (PDF)
ISBN 978-3-593-44328-7 E-Book (EPUB)

Cover design: Guido Klütsch, Köln
Design and Typesetting: Publikations Atelier, Dreieich
Printing office and bookbinder: Beltz Bad Langensalza GmbH
Printed in Germany

www.campus.de

CONTENTS

INTRODUCTION

In the world of information technology, every effort is made to keep computer systems free of viruses and malware. Their dangers are obvious, which is why systems and networks must be secured. The best way to do so is by continual updates, allowing computers to correct themselves, repair damage, and learn to deal with threats.

But how to prevent "viruses" from infesting the thoughts and ideas of human beings? How to prevent "malware" in the form of misguided ideas and dangerous misconceptions from entering our heads – and particularly the heads of executives in societies' countless organizations? How can we prevent the functioning of our organizations being "hacked"? A still more important question is: How can the thinking of executives be provided with the right updates, containing the concepts that point the future?

What's new doesn't have a name yet

These questions are important because we are witnesses to the emergence of a New World. Economy and society are undergoing one of the greatest transformations in history. The Old World, as we knew it, is turning into a New World, which we still can know only in outline, and in some of its rudiments. We can conjecture a little more, from which we can infer that in this New World, nearly everything will be unlike it is today.

The greatest challenge is to move from the Old World to the New, for in the period of transition, the Old World will keep functioning *less and less*, while the New World is *not yet* up and running. Since 1997, I have been referring to this process of profound change as "The Great Transformation21" and offered a detailed discussion of it in my books. In order to describe it, I needed a largely new language – that of cybernetics, from which the term "governance" is borrowed. The language of the Old World masks and distorts nearly all the New World's important traits, precisely because they are new. In fact, we probably do not yet even have words for what may turn out to be the crucial properties of the New World. In times of transition, we are in particular danger of failing to notice such properties until we are suddenly confronted with them.

Such was also the case with earlier transitions. What was new did not have a name. After all, what to call an apparatus able to do something that, according to the "laws of nature," *was not even possible*? The Germans came upon the imaginative idea of calling it *Flugzeug* or "flying-tool." The English word *aeroplane* (or, in American usage, *airplane*), derived from the French *aéro* and the Greek *planos*, "wandering," seems more lyrical, but similarly baffled by the sheer novelty of what it seeks to describe. If we tried to describe today's computerized world in terms of the mechanized office of the 1960s, we would struggle to understand computers.

Nearly everything is going to change

Many of the terms used today are "dangerous" because they describe the new wrongly, because they prevent its understanding and thus impede progress. For nearly everything will change in the course of the Great Transformation21: *what* we do, *why* we do it, and *how* we do it – and consequently also *who* we are. One day, we may look back on it as the most profound transformation in history, greater that the Industrial Revolution, than the Renaissance and Reformation, and the earlier transformations of the thirteenth century. The Great Transformation21 is taking place all over the world and affects all areas of society, above all its millions of organizations.

The Great Transformation21 is driven by four principal forces, which join to form a new reality. The most important drivers are technology, particularly digitalization and biotechnologies, the profound changes in the demographic makeup of most modern states, the global ecological challenges as well as the global economy and above all its debt. These four forces are closely interconnected. They influence, reinforce, modify, and hasten each other. From their interconnection, a new, all-encompassing reality emerges: exponentially growing, dynamic, and self-reinforcing complexity on a scale hitherto unknown.

The more complex the world becomes and the more it changes, the clearer our thinking needs to be if it is to help us find our way. And the clearer must also be the language and terminology that enable us to communicate effectively.

What we already know

What can we already know about the Great Transformation21 today? After all, it is not beginning only now, nor did it begin only with the iPhone. A more useful date might be 1994, when Netscape released the first web browser accessible to non-specialists and inaugurated the internet as we know it – the General Public Internet, as it were. Previously, only specialists or enthusiastic hobbyists had used it. The scientific foundations for the Great Transformation21 were already laid in the late 1940s by Cybernetics, which studied nature's third fundamental entity: information.

We know that the new society is at once a knowledge society, an organization society, and a complexity society. We know that it needs to be an effectively functioning society and that, in order to be so, it needs effectively functioning organizations. And thus, we also know that it will be a society in which management will be the key function, and that such management must be of the systems-cybernetic kind, based on sciences of complexity – on systems theory, cybernetics, and bionics. On account of their inherent risks, some types of organization began early on to work systematically to achieve ever better functioning, among them airports and hospitals.

In a world of functioning, the previous ideologies will be of little significance, for they are typically Old World modes of thought. Just as the natural sciences were never socialist, capitalist, or imperialist – or Catholic, or Buddhist –, the functioning of organizations, too, will come to be considered outside any ideological framework. Yet perhaps it will bring forth a meta-philosophy of applied *functionism*, as I have suggested in several of my books: by functioning management for functioning organizations. Only thus will true leadership be possible for the first time.

Effective communication will be decisive for functioning societies in the New World, at the level of computer networks, and of organizations and the people working in them. A functioning language may thus turn out to be crucial to the New World and its functioning. This does not pose much of a problem for computer networks, which have always made use of the cybernetic properties of feedback networks to correct themselves, have long worked with "Double Loop Feedback" and, in doing so, became self-teaching systems. Much greater difficulties are faced by people – not people taken by themselves, but people in organizations.

More than the finer points of language

Language exerts a decisive influence on perception, thought, communication, and action. Language is the foundation of right leadership, and language is the tool of those who use it to mislead. My concern in this book is with neither the finer points of usage nor questions of style or preference, but with right thinking and effective communication *in management*. But this is not an issue just of lucidity and concision. It is easy to put the greatest nonsense in clear and simple terms. All some people need is 280 characters and a few hashtags. Clarity has nothing to do with a statement's inherent accuracy.

At stake are clarity, accuracy, and professional precision. "Dangerous" words are sources of misunderstanding. They impede accurate understanding and sensible communication. They lead to misguided expectations and wrong behavior in people and organizations.

A clear and precise terminology is the hallmark of developed sciences and disciples. Professionalism and competence depend on a command of the core concepts. Nobody in a scientific or technical discipline could expect to be taken seriously without grasping the distinction between speed and acceleration. A lawyer unaware of the difference between possession and ownership would be not just incompetent, but dangerous. Precision is key when subtle but important decisions are at stake.

Analogous problems are not a rarity, but a common occurrence in management, where we are still far from the precision and clarity long ago attained by and indeed taken for granted in advanced disciplines. In virtually every discussion, my experience is that executives, as professional as they may be in their respective specializations, either lack a clear sense of the meaning of certain terms or assume that the same clarity obtains in management as it does it their own disciplines. As a consequence of this assumption, they are often surprised to find themselves in a linguistic quagmire.

14

The most dangerous word in this collection – and the most endangered?

Of all the "dangerous words in management" collected here, barely any single one is misunderstood as often as *management* itself. Major uncertainty exists as to what management actually is, what it is not, and what it ought to be. This is the main source of misunderstanding and error, and the reason for the slow advance of this practical discipline, for the recurring fads plaguing the profession, and for the Babylonian confusion and disorientation in which so many people feel stuck.

It is also one of the principal reasons for the animosity – often latent but increasingly open – and indeed hostility toward management and managers. In my work as teacher, coach, and adviser to executives, I was nearly always able soon to ensure clarity and to reduce or assuage such antipathy by means of the distinction between right and wrong, good and bad management that I have developed over decades.

Right and good management I take to be the societal function that allows a society's organizations and systems to function in a right and good manner. That is why, in this new edition, I have decided to include the worst misunderstandings surrounding the concept of management itself.

In this book, I address a selection of words whose careless use I regard as a widespread habit as well as often being, in the sense outlined above, dangerous, confusing, or deceptive. Examples are *charisma* or *gut feeling*. Others are words – *motivation*, for instance – around which a misguided practice or comprehensive misjudgments – as in the case of *emotion* – have accrued. Such words have been so much used in recent years that they have entered the standard vocabulary of management and appear to have a clear meaning. In this *apparent* clarity and *apparent* intelligibility there lie dangers.

In part, these words are the expression and consequence of fads. Indeed, few other areas are as prone to the vagaries of fashion as management. But to a large extent the words addressed here are also the consequence of insufficient or one-sided training in management. The "danger" of these terms goes beyond that of general miscommunication. They steer thought in action in wrong directions. They transport ideas about leading businesses, treating employees, and dealing with customers that are harmful and can sometimes lead businesses to collapse.

The terms I class as "dangerous" are put to numerous purposes. They are uses to shape opinion and policy, to do business, to bolster interests, and to legitimize status. They are also terms that are used to impress. Trying to impress is the strategy of a particular kind of expert. To create an impression is their crucial means of making a living – after all, they have no other. That is why they will do anything to maintain semantic illusions. Their tools of choice are cloudy language, high-flown terminology, and fashionable but empty phrases. Yet good executives are not so easily impressed, but demand precise knowledge. They use the strongest heuristic device to obtain it. They ask, *well, is any of that right?*

Knowledge can help guard against most mistakes and immunize against fads. It saves time and money, the laborious learning and unlearning of misconceptions. Each of the words discussed here represents a moment of imprecision, a logical fallacy, a misguided theory, or a widespread but erroneous opinion in management – and to correct them is to work on the bridge leading to the New World, to contribute to better, functioning, and responsible management.

I wish to thank Tamara Bechter for her uniquely sensitive contributions to this new edition's conception, style, and content, Selina Hartmann at Campus Verlag for taking good care of the manuscript and Joe Kroll for his unmistakable feeling for the subtleties of the English language which is just for this text so important.

St. Gallen, Switzerland, September 2019

CHARISMA

"We need charismatic leaders!" is a demand that recurs periodically, and in recent times quite emphatically. Little wonder, for we face great challenges. Of course, it is not enough for managers to be able to read and write and otherwise be averagely decent human beings. But why fall into the opposite extreme? Somehow, an idea has taken hold that managers, especially those at the top, ought to be a mix of a Nobel Prize winner, a Roman military commander, and a TV personality: a jack-of-all-trades, if you will, or the perfect Renaissance man.

We have learned to tolerate, or rather to suffer, a great deal of nonsense in connection with management. But to add charisma makes the nonsense dangerous. In the light of the experiences of the twentieth century, should we not be a little more careful what we wish for? Was not the last century that of consummate charismatic leaders – Hitler, Stalin, and Mao? Are we safe in the knowledge that such history will not repeat itself, is over and done with?

I am far from denying the effect charismatic leaders have on people. But this is precisely why what matters is not *that* we are led, but *where*. The effect of leaders is important. It must be tempered with responsibility. Historically, charismatic leaders have all too often wreaked disaster – in so many fields.

Charismatic leaders can be dangerous because, knowing the effect they have, they flout rules. They can be unpredictable and pursue utopias. Charismatic leaders are as likely to *mis*lead, to lead *astray*, as they are to lead well. Real leaders who successfully overcome even the greatest and hardest challenges do so not by depending on charisma. They lead by self-discipline and example, not by sloganeering and bluster. Their capital is not charisma, but trust.

At the head of organizations, it can sometimes be important and often advantageous, although not absolutely essential, to exert a pull over people. Charismatic personalities can always be a risk factor, too. Indeed, the very clamor for "great" leadership figures can be dangerous. The few to have been not only great, but also good leaders are exceptions. They can all too easily lead us to overlook the many excellent executives at the head of thousands of organizations necessary to the functioning of economy and society.

LEADERSHIP

Leadership fascinates. That is why it is important to distinguish the fads from the real substance. For most people, leadership hinges on personality. That is where the source of leadership is supposed to be, and from there personal fascination emanates. But this is exactly what distracts from the matter of real importance: to look closely at what actual leaders are *doing*, and *how* they are doing it. For this reason, I distinguish – as discussed above – between "real leaders" and "mis-leaders". After the disasters into which leaders led humanity in the twentieth century, we should know better than to accept a notion of leadership blind to history. And is not without reason that in German, the English *leader* has largely supplanted the all too familiar word *Führer*.

In history, successful leaders in politics and business have displayed very different personalities. One trait they shared was effectiveness, for even the best properties are of no consequence if they cannot be converted into actual performance and results. Rhetoric and showmanship will not suffice in the long term. To make leadership effective, effective management is needed, which is founded on *knowledge* and *experience* – and talent is a welcome addition. Leaders, too, cannot do without management. Often, they are themselves good managers and have effective managers in their teams, though they will not leave it at that.

Real leaders concentrate on the task, not their own needs

Real leaders do not ask, *what do I want, what would suit me?*, but *what needs to be done in this situation for the benefit of all?* They are not guided by potential rewards for themselves, but see the duty to master a situation in which they often find themselves by accident – to avert danger or to seize an opportunity. They accept their own insignificance relative to the task in hand. They put themselves at the service of the objective. In doing so, they earn trust, respect, and approval. The internal stance of privileging the task ahead of oneself allows real leaders to display courage and character in decisive moments, particularly when they are forced to decide between the importance of the task on the one hand and their own careers on the other. In the worst case, leaders will sacrifice their careers for the sake of the matter in hand. Nothing could better persuade others that such leaders really mean what they say.

Real leaders are result-oriented

Words are not enough, though leaders are often able to deploy them masterfully. If results fail to materialize, they will not seek refuge in threadbare excuses, for they know their credibility to be on the line. Here, we can easily identify the juncture at which the downfall of so many historical personalities began: their leadership began to lose its luster when they started to cover up their failures with alibis and excuses, or to lay blame on scapegoats and imaginary conspiracies.

Real leaders force themselves to listen

"Force themselves" should be emphasized, for few find it easy. Many leaders are impatient because they are convinced that their actions are, at heart, right. Yet they also know just how important this makes the information that they cannot themselves obtain, particularly that from the bottom of their organizations. Time and again, they muster the will, the time, and the self-discipline to listen – because they know that otherwise, they stand to lose their organization's trust. Often, they listen only briefly, for they are usually pressed for time. But in that short time, they are noticeably attentive.

Real leaders make themselves understood

They know that what is obvious to themselves – their views, their ideas and imaginings – are by no means as clear to others, nor, as a rule, can they be. That's why they are constantly working on making themselves understood by others. They tirelessly restate their core messages, again and again, patiently and tenaciously. To make themselves understood, they deploy clear language. Often, they avail themselves of the clearest means of communication of all: They demonstrate what they mean. They lead by example.

We, not I

For all their well-earned achievements and all their conviction of being abler than others in many respects, real leaders will not take credit on behalf of others. They think in terms of we, not I. They understand the contributions made by their employees and the organization as a whole, and they recognize them. Their concern is with the success of their cause, not their own personal success.

Unafraid of strong people

This applies in all direction, with regard to superiors and inferiors, equals and colleagues. Leaders know that only the best people are capable of meeting an organization's big challenges. Therefore, they will do anything to attract the best people, to support and promote them, and to set them to work where they are needed most. They may respond in a tough, even harsh manner to attempts at undermining their authority. But they will not eliminate string people out of fear for their own position. To gather weaklings, favorites, and yes-men around oneself is a sure sign of weak leadership, and can often be detected early on. Real leaders don't care for yes-men who parrot their every word.

Leaders can be inspiring individuals – but they don't have to be

One constantly hears the demand for leaders to be inspiring individuals, able to arouse enthusiasm in others. This is a misconception, for inspiration and enthusiasm are decisive obstacles to leadership in truly critical situations. The call for inspiration is obviously made with only the positive and easy leadership situations in mind. But real leadership comes into its own in difficult situations, in which unpopular and tough sacrifices are demanded of people. As long as it is easy to win people over to the matter in hand, there is little need for true leadership. Rhetoric and showmanship will usually be enough.

Leadership is situational

Leadership is not an absolute, but depends on a situation and can be understood and explained only with reference to that situation. People who are thought of as leaders confront the challenge posed by situations in which they often find themselves only by accident. They assume responsibility, look for solutions, and act. Leadership resides not in their person alone, perhaps even not foremost. It is the situation and the specific actions taken in that situation that together constitute leadership. Without that situation, the actions referred to as leadership would be neither necessary nor sensible. Be it a crisis or an opportunity: It is the situation that separates the leader from the showman.

Management is not leadership

For some time now, a stark divide between management on the one hand and leadership on the other has brought forth a tide of confusion, in which learning about either becomes nearly impossible: The rubric "management" is made to encompass all the ill-regarded and "lowly" tasks such as running day-to-day business, taking care of operational matters, planning, controlling, and budgeting. In this view, managers are seen principally as blinkered bureaucrats. "Leadership," on the other hand, comes to comprise all that is good and fair, forward-looking, future-oriented, innovative, and visionary, and thus everything considered desirable. Everyone is free to see things in this manner, but doing so adds no knowledge, only confusion.

Management certainly involves the ability to lead, but not leadership in the sense discussed here. If we are to understand the distinctive property of management, it is more instructive to imagine management in positive terms and then to ask what it takes above and beyond that. That could then be real and truly good leadership: Something exceeding even the best management. Yet on the other hand, leadership cannot be effective without the help of professional management – least of all in a world that is becoming increasingly complex.

LEADERSHIP STYLE

The right leadership style is among the most discussed questions of recent decades. There can hardly be a subject to which so much empirical research has been devoted, and there can barely be an executive who has not thought about this question. No executive training program would be complete without it. Yet I tend to consider the subject largely unimportant, or at any rate far less important than it is usually held to be. For this opinion, completely at odds with contemporary wisdom, I have two reasons:

No correlation

First, there is no correlation between style and outcomes. It may of course be possible to produce correlations under laboratory conditions: Every coach knows exercises by which to achieve that goal. They are standard on the seminar circuit, and are good for producing insights and communicating lessons. But they are not applicable to the reality of business. The "bridge building" exercise, for instance, is often set up in such a way to let the cooperative group win. That's fine as long there is no engineer or skilled artisan in the group.

We all know people who cultivate a cooperative leadership style and at the same time produce excellent results. That situation is the optimum. On the other hand, there are executives who lead in an authoritarian fashion and produce poor results. This situation is equally clear: It is intolerable, and it may be necessary to let such people go. Neither case offers much scope for disagreement.

But most people will also know executives who lead cooperatively and are extremely likable and cultured – yet to little avail. And then there are managers who lead by directive, strictly, and thus are often thought authoritarian, yet have excellent results to show for it. Given the choice, I would always go for the second type.

Manners matter

My second argument is that style doesn't matter. But something else does, something that is hardly ever mentioned in management training: manners. One might also call it civility or decency. Whenever I say this, somebody is sure to tell me that that's precisely what they mean by style. But style and manners are not the same thing. This is not a question of highly developed rituals of ceremonious politeness, but elementary good form. It's a matter of simple things, saying "please" and "thank you," letting people finish their sentences, listening to them, not interrupting, not yelling, not being moody or taking it out on others. Manners, in short, that one should have learned in childhood, but if, as an executive, one has to deal with people who did not, then one must demand they make an effort in the workplace and brook no compromise in this question. Boorish behavior will not be tolerated. This has little to do with style, and a lot with correctness. No amount of style will compensate for a lack of correctness.

No career for ruffians

Manners are not the fuel, not the source of energy that propels and organization. But they are the lubricant that makes everyday friction bearable. Where decency is lacking, no amount of training in conflict management will help. Conflict management should thus not be the first step. The prime task is not to resolve conflicts, but do deal with people in such a way as to prevent conflict from occurring in the first place. One precondition for this is manners. There is a place for protocol and etiquette, and the higher up one goes, the less one can afford to ignore them. But they are seldom decisive in conducting everyday business. Manners and decency, on the other hand, are.

ECONOMIC ACTIVITY

The main reason for our work is often simply overlooked and seems to be completely unfamiliar to some. In consequence, the essential core of "economic activity" is not understood – a failure that poses real dangers as soon as far-reaching reforms become necessary with respect to supposedly secure possessions of the affluent society. Why do humans work? Why do they even engage in economic activity?

Work and economic activity are consistently explained in terms of human will and striving: people, in this account, want to satisfy their needs. As consumers, they seek utility or the fulfillment of desire. As entrepreneurs, they want to make a profit, or grow, or both. As employees, they work because they have been motivated. As managers, they want to be productive and innovative.

Why we engage in economic activity

These commonly cited driving forces of economic activity are clearly psychological in nature. That doesn't just sound plausible, it's largely the dominant doctrine. But is this really the case? Do such subjective elements of wanting, wishing, and striving truly explain the pressure felt within the economy? Why should one face this pressure rather than avoiding or ignoring it? The answer is: because of competition.

The common perception of economics overlooks by far the most important point: people work, and entrepreneurs and businesses engage in economic activity, not because the *want* to do so, but because they *have to*. They act under compulsion. This follows from the fact – as simple as it compelling – that individuals and corporations enter obligations that are fixed in their scope and duration and that must be fulfilled. In brief: they have debts.

Some debt relations are entered into freely and might thus be avoided. The associated acts of purchase – be they payable by installments, credit cards, or leasing rates – might after all be postponed. But once debts have been incurred, their effect is unrelenting and irreversible: They must be paid, and not just the original loan, but also any interest agreed upon. Such obligations may be entered into voluntarily; their repayment is binding.

Is that the whole truth?

Taken alone, this would not be enough to understand economics. By far the greater part of debt contracts in entered into *involuntarily*. All production and all work need to be financed in advance. Buyers will buy only once production has started, and pay paid out only after work has begun. Pre-financing inevitably leads to debt contracts and to additional costs known as interest.

The debtor is thus forced – regardless of his striving, desire, or motivation – not only to produce repayment of the loan, i.e. to render a service that he might possibly

31

not have rendered but for the existence of the debt contract. (But for the obligation, he might after all just have taken the time off.) The debtor must furthermore produce a surplus in the size of the interest owed.

We hear little of this cause of economic activity, its characteristically hectic pace and constant pressure – surprisingly, given that global debt is higher than ever in both relative and absolute terms. Low interest rates may, for the time being, make this burden more bearable. Yet the commitment to additional production is, in absolute figures, quite staggering. This driving force behind economic activity is altogether independent of psychological motives and any other goals, desires, and plans.

Understanding economic activity

The sum of all obligations multiplied by the applicable interest rate corresponds to the total economic surplus output necessary to avert collapse. We owe this insight tone of the best economists I know, Paul C. Martin.[1] Taking his cue from the works of Gunnar Heinsohn and Otto Steiger,[2] his contributions were crucial to developing the so-called debitist theory of economics, without which there can be no understanding of how the economy works.

We are accustomed to dividing people into certain categories: consumers and producers, employers and employees. They are far from irrelevant, but they explain comparatively little. Far more important are the categories of debtor and creditor.

In this debitist view, the market is not just the place where supply and demand meet. It is above all the place where indebted producers try to obtain the requisite means to cover their debts, i.e. money. By no means is capitalism a system devoted to maximizing profit, nor can it be understood based on that principle. It may seem so from a contemplative perspective removed from real economic life. In capitalism, it is wholly irrelevant whether someone makes a profit or not. Capitalism is a system in which bills must be paid. That is the only valid definition. Ultimately, solvency is the key, not profit. The debtor pays his bills for as long as he can. And when he is no longer able, the creditor pays by writing off the irrecoverable claim. It is not the usual expectations or the constantly invoked psychological factors (important though they are) that are the decisive element in understanding economic activity. People would be able to wind down their expectations for their everyday lives quite far – but for their debts. The fall in share and property prices would be of concern to no-one – had they not been bought on credit. Recovery, therefore, does not begin in the head. It begins and ends with debt.

DOING BUSINESS

A common misapprehension regarding the connection between economic activity and management is the opinion that management is chiefly a matter of business, that only businesses need to be managed, or that management was developed in business.

Management is frequently seen as something crudely materialistic, and often it is dismissed as mere "wheeling and dealing" or profiteering. While it is true that the word "management" is often used when doing business is the issue – be it shady deals or the activity of honest merchants – there is a considerable difference between businesspeople and entrepreneurs, and another difference between an entrepreneur and an enterprise. Yet management is something altogether different. Management is a universal social function. It is needed in all of society's institutions. That is why it is far too important a matter for superficial errors and misconceptions to be left casually unchallenged.

Management is not limited to business

Maybe it is in business that the effects of management are the most visible. One reason is that businesses produce figure of a kind unavailable in other organizations. In business, much can be measured that is not quantifiable elsewhere. The effects of management errors soon show up in the statistics, and they do so sooner than in other organizations. But that doesn't mean that the fatal consequences of wrong or poor management are not visible in other organizations: a patient undergoing an operation on the wrong leg; a student not taught to read and write properly … Of course, companies need to do business, they need orders and sales. But these are not the activities I call "management," by which I mean the leadership of the organization engaged in business. The leadership of an organization with a set task to fulfill.

Management is not business studies or business administration

The kind of knowledge taught in a business studies course alone will never be enough to lead a business. It required additional and different knowledge of a kind that so far has not found its way into business studies curricula – which is not intended as a criticism, but simply reflects the disciplinary boundaries as we find them. I am far from denying that theoretical knowledge of business is important in leading a business. But that is not the case, to the same extent, for the management of other organizations. The spread of MBA programs has given rise to the perception that they somehow constituted the apex of management training. This, too, is a misapprehension. Management is as little identical with business studies as it is with business administration. All organizations may need to be managed, but not all require a background in business studies or business administration in order to do so. In fact, only a minority do, and some would suffer

grievous harm from being managed under purely business aspects – be they symphony orchestras, schools, or
healthcare providers.

MANAGING AND LEADING PEOPLE

Another widespread opinion is that management consists primarily or even exclusively of managing and leading people. This error can be traced to the fact that the term "leadership" has never been so naturally applied to the management of an institution as a whole as it is to the management of individuals, groups, or teams. Now, management includes leading people, but is far more still. In the absence of an understanding that management must also be applied to the institution as a whole, then the understanding of management as leading people will also take a wrong turn.

This attitude ignores that leading people does not refer to the leadership of people *qua* people, but of *people in organizations*. That is matter quite apart from people in their private lives. At the same time, it is liable to produce a one-sidedly rationalistic view of organizations. It is all too easy to ignore that both aspects depend on each other: At stake is the leadership of people in organizations, and *the formation of organizations with people*.

That is one reason why this is a difficult task. Each taken on its own would be relatively easy to solve; taken together, they pose difficult questions. This leads us to a further problem. If leading people is not seen as indissolubly linked with the functional requirements of organizations, then one runs the risk of applying things that are important to the private lives of people to organizations, where they are often completely misplaced. Much of the motivation industry suffers from this fault, but it also affects other areas, for instance the question whether a job can or ought to be fun.

Conversely, principles indispensable to people in organizations, which otherwise would cease to function, should not be thoughtlessly applied to private life, where they do not belong and can be harmful.

MANAGEMENT

Confusion is still rife as to what management actually is, ought to be, and on no account should be. With the increasing importance of management, countless concepts and ideas relating to it have entered circulation. Many of them are not just misleading, but simply nonsensical, and testify to a lack of understanding of this practical discipline.

Distinguishing management from the operational level

Misunderstandings often emerge from the conflation of management tasks and specialized or operational tasks. The divisions typical of commercial enterprises – research and development, marketing, manufacturing, finances, accounts, human resources etc.–are frequently treated as management tasks. In fact, however, these are specific operational or specialist tasks, and require the technical and specialist knowledge to be carried out properly.

A graduate of a course in marketing, finance, accounting, or the like will (it is to be hoped) end up an expert in that field, but is still far from being a manager. Management is faced with different tasks, for instance, to set goals, to organize, decide, control, to develop people. To perform specific operational tasks well requires management. And conversely, management cannot be pursued irrespective of a task in hand. Management is always management *of something*.

A societal function

Right and good management I take to be the social function that allows a society's organizations and systems to function in a right and good manner. Management is the driving force wherever goals can be reached only jointly, by many individuals interconnecting their work and knowledge. Management is the organ of leadership in all a society's organizations – in a commercial enterprise as well as in a non-profit organization, in the administration of a country or a town, in a university or a hospital.

Management decisions and processes give organizations purpose, values, and direction, and they determine their missions and goals. Management mobilizes the necessary resources and converts them into results serving a larger purpose. In order to do so, management must be effective and efficient. This means that it must do the right things, and do them well. Management thus understood comprises leadership and governance. It comprises enabling people to contribute to the proper functioning of their organizations. Such management creates orientation, structure, and the potential for performance. In doing so, it also answers to a social, political, and ethical responsibility.

Mastering complexity

Among the greatest challenges facing management today are the dynamic of change in economy and society and the exponentially growing complexity resulting from the global interconnection of ever more spheres of life. That is why I take management also to mean mastering complexity. The scientific grounding for properly functioning management systems is thus to be found in the sciences of complexity, in systemics, cybernetics, and bionics. Systemics I define as the study of coherent entities, cybernetics as the science of functioning, and bionics means the transference of solutions optimized by natural evolution to social organizations. Only these sciences can produce conceptual clarity where today confusion, contradiction, and fads dominate management. These sciences enable the use of diversity, of self-regulation and self-organization, of evolutionary processes for organizations' leaning and their adaptability.

The profession of effectiveness and the path to viability

Managers – or "executives"–are individuals who embody management as a societal function and who make a profession of this function. Thus understood, management is also the *profession of effectiveness* in organizations. Right management and self-management are as important for the people of the 21st century as reading and writing became for their ancestors in the seventeenth century. Management skills today represent the key competency that makes people employable and effective in organizations. In all organizations, professional success is increasingly the consequence of right and good management. For only thus can – beyond economic resources –

talent, skills, intelligence, and creativity be made usable. Only thus are information, knowledge, and insight transformed into results.

Management for people and management for organizations are the two key dimensions of the application of effective management systems. Only by right and good management can people convert their strengths into performance, be successful, and find purpose in life through their effective actions. Right and good management makes people fit for life and organizations able to function.

CULTURE

It is striking how often everything that goes wrong in an organization is blamed on culture –"lacking," "poor," or "wrong" corporate culture. Organizational culture currently is the handy scapegoat for everything that "isn't functioning right." But malfunctions in organizations can be down to many other reasons: bad or wrong strategy, for instance, inappropriate structures, bad staffing decisions, and insufficient or simply wrong management skills. Yet organizational culture has come to be the catch-all term for all errors and defects. How come?

Misleading solutions

One of the main reasons is the failure to distinguish between the two entirely different levels on which an organization's activities take place. On the one hand there is the *operational level*, the level on which an organization performs the specialist task for which it was founded: building cars, for instance, healing patients, educating students. On the other hand, there is the *management* level, that of steering, controlling, and regulating. This is the level that ensure the functioning of the operational level.

At the operational level, organizations, and commercial enterprises in particular, can and must be – for strategic reasons – very *different*, and at that level will have correspondingly different cultures. Their competitiveness depends on it. The cultural values in the hotel business will be very different depending on whether we look at a three-star or a five-star establishment. The same applies in retail, the airline industry – everywhere. But at the management level, all well-functioning organizations are the same. The management level is that of *functioning*. Both three- and five-star hotels have to function correctly, well, and reliably – indeed perfectly – within their respective ecosystems. This is where the values of *effective* and *right* management apply, and these values are the same for all organizations. There is only *one* way for an organization to function, whereas there are thousands of varieties of poor functioning. The many kinds of poor functioning provide a valuable resource for studies of organizational culture, in master's and doctoral theses.

The *what* of right management is very similar across all cultures. Yet *how* something is done can differ wildly, and usually does. In every well-run organization – not, by contrast, in those that are poorly run – one finds, for instance, clear goals, right decisions, good personnel development, functioning communication, effective meetings and reliable control, regardless of whether the company is Italian, German, or Chinese. Appearances vary; the purpose is the same.

The culture of functioning

Management is right or wrong, good or bad, able or inept. Is it as little dependent on culture as is competing successfully in sport. The crucial point is that there are always far more ways of doing it wrong than doing it right. Bad management comes in so many forms because everyone acts wrongly in their particular way. The scope of good management, on the other hand, is much narrower. If you want to do it right, golf is played in exactly the same way across the world, as are tennis or chess. There are many wrong ways to play golf, but only one is right. By the same token, the rules of effectiveness and professionalism in management apply equally everywhere.

From this result the values of the *culture of functioning*. It constitutes a new ethics for organizations, which begins to take effect when people in an organization are guided by the following values: *results, contribution to the whole, concentration, strengths, trust, positive thinking, innovation, purpose*. These are the cultural values of what, in the introduction to this book, I called the new functionism. They are the same the world over – as long as organizations work. The many applications of right management may then still require additional skills, for instance knowledge of foreign languages or of local history and manners. But the foundation consists of management knowledge and management skills acquired once and perfected continually – on this basis, a culture of reliable functioning can be built.

FUNCTIONING

To many, "functioning," particularly in relation to people, carries an extremely negative connotation. After all, nobody wants "merely to function" as a human being. Of our organizations, however, we should demand just that: the ability to function as reliably and as flawlessly as possible. That is also why functioning is my most general term for *the reliable and optimum working of an organization according to its purpose.* An organization's ability to function is not the same as a person's adaptedness to life. Especially in management, we need to make a clear distinction here.

Remarkably enough, most people have little trouble seeing what *does not* work in an organization. Things that function wrongly, insufficiently, or not all call our attention to themselves. Yet especially in management, we would do well to pay attention to what function particularly well and without friction, and to look for the roots of this ability and learn from it.

For it with this knowledge in mind that we can go one step further to the meta-property of *viability.* Viability means an organization's ability to support its functioning indefinitely. To give an example: When a resource approaches exhaustion, a system must be capable of adapting to another resource and to prepare the transition in good time. Viability means more than sustainability. An organization's functioning must include the capacity *to adapt to unprecedented events.*

NEW WORK

I am constantly being asked what's new in management – as I have been for some 40 years. True enough, in this time, I have witnessed a new fad in management on average every two or three years: a new approach, a new topic about which everyone was suddenly abuzz, a new wave of seminars, and a flood of books seemingly written overnight. After a couple of years, the wave recedes, only to be followed little later by the next. In the meantime, tens of thousands of managers across the length and breadth of the country are sent, with the best of intentions, to attend seminars in "new management."

Just new or actually right?

Few academic disciplines are as subject to fashion as management is, because unlike management they allow for errors to be exposed and corrected by criticism. This engine of progress – institutionalized, systematic criticism – is almost entirely absent from management. Other disciplines continually build on earlier findings, whereas in management, the most important goal is usually perceived as creating something "entirely new." A book on management that is more than three years old tends to be regarded as hopelessly outdated.

"New Work" is just a small part of a far larger New World that – advancing by leaps and bounds – is in the process of displacing the Old World. Now more than ever, since we are living through a time of fundamental change, we should scrutinize developments carefully. For only a few years hence, nearly everything will be unlike it is today: *what we do, how we do it, why we do it – and also who we are*. "New Workers" already are the knowledge workers of whom we need more and more, and urgently. With their knowledge, they in turn convert knowledge into knowledge. For knowledge workers, practically everything is different from the way it was for the workers of old. They are their own bosses. They own their means of production and they take them home at night. It's not even certain that they'll be back the next day.

Doing the right things right

Instead of "New Work," we would do better to speak of Knowledge Work. Doing so makes clear what is important and what will become increasingly important. Knowledge Work transforms knowledge into utility; it is always interconnected, and ever more frequently acts to interconnect. Time and space cease to matter to the knowledge worker. *But the crucial point is not what is "new" about this, but how what is new becomes efficacious. Effectiveness* is the ability on the part of people and organizations to do the *right* things. *Efficiency* is the ability to do them well. Taken together, they produce the efficacy needed to obtain results. It is efficacy that defines professionalism – not novelty value.

MAKING MISTAKES

Are we *allowed* to make mistakes? *Ought* one to make mistakes, is it perhaps even a *necessity*? The call for a new "Failure Culture" in businesses is quite recent. It is not yet being raised with regard to other organizations, for instance hospitals, where mistakes might have the most immediate and severe impact on health and life of human beings. Yet making mistakes has advanced with surprising rapidity to the rank of a much-discussed cultural buzzword. Do we need to take this development seriously, or is it just a welcome excuse for sloppiness? In fact, we should take it seriously, but not confuse it with sloppiness. Agile methods in particular, often radically departing from the waterfall model of old, call for a new failure culture, the better to master the ever more complex tasks in IT and software development. A rigid, non-adaptable process is supplanted by the logic of trial and error. This is clearly of tremendous benefit to many IT projects and hence to be welcomed.

Trial and error: the logic of evolution

The logic of evolution is a wonderful process – if we have no other choice. And it's not altogether new, but about 4 billion years old. Trial and error is both ideal and inevitable when we have no prior knowledge, when we break new ground – because we have to continue past the point where the beaten track stops. Paths are created by walking, and in doing so, errors are inevitable. This is one of the fundamental logics of systems-cybernetic management that help master great complexity intelligently.[3]

Trial and error is a heuristic principle for navigation. Heuristics is the big sister to the algorithms ubiquitous in today's digitalizing world. Heuristics provide step-by-step instructions for finding the direction and proximity of a goal that cannot be exactly located. We may know *what* the goal is, but not *where* it might be found. Unlike ransom search processes, heuristics help reach an unknown goal by means of *rule-guided exploration* or *targeted experimentation*. Mistakes are understood as signaling a need for corrections. Broadly speaking, the heuristic might be expressed as "trial – error – new trial – new error" etc., until a provisional solution has been found from which to continue the search.

There is every reason to demand a better way of dealing with mistakes where leadership is ossified and bureaucratized. Yet it is worth being skeptical as to whether the "failure" culture celebrated in start-up circles really is the panacea for good leadership it is sometimes hyped as.

For there are two sides to making mistakes, one innovative and one destructive. It is important to distinguish *when* and *where* it is permissible to make mistakes, and particularly *to what end*. I distinguish three fundamentally different situations: mistakes in operating business, mistakes in innovations, and mistakes in transformations and while navigating into the unknown.

No license to slip up

Would you fly an airline that is proud of its pilots' errors? Would you enroll your children at a school whose stated principles include the right to make mistakes? The answer will inevitably be, "well, of course that's not *quite* what I had in mind." But then, what? Some people will try to differentiate: It's fine to make mistakes, but never the same one twice. That sounds much better – but is it good enough? Are there not mistakes that must never be made, not even once? How many times is it acceptable for a pharmacist to dispense the wrong medication, for a surgeon to botch an operation? Another variant runs: It's fine to make mistakes if you can learn from them. That principle, too, cannot apply without qualification. After all, no lesson learned will bring comfort to a patient who has not received the right treatment.

That mistakes will happen, that they occur even under the very best management, is a fact we have to live with. But this acknowledgement should not be read as giving *carte blanche* to a "failure culture," let alone taking pride in and to propagating it as a special advance in management.

The better rule

Mistakes are not acceptable. That is the foundation of right and good management, the default principle – particularly in operating business, particularly where organizations must work well and reliably every day. Only once this foundation has been accepted is it possible to make distinctions: For instance, of course a company's R&D department must be given the license to experiment. But that has little to do with "it's fine to make mistakes" in the sense discussed here. Experiments take place *under controlled conditions* in order to prevent mistakes having severe consequences.

It is equally obvious that mistakes are to be expected from beginners and where people are trained or learn on the job, wherever experience is to be gathered. The sensible rule is that this should happen away from the operating business or under supervision and instruction, until such time as one can be certain that no further mistakes will be made, for that is the purpose of training. Here, too, it would be rather questionable to say, "Make mistakes, or you won't learn anything!" In management training, in particular, I do not believe that mistakes require any special pleading. After all, here it is possible to make good progress just by learning and thinking – which is a great advantage we in management enjoy. In positions of leadership, this comes with the obligation constantly and thoroughly to reflect, question, and analyze critically.

How to deal with mistakes

In most of a modern society's professions, mistakes are simply not acceptable. Talk of a positive or negative culture of failure changes nothing about this principle. It applies to heart surgeons, accountants, and pilots. Why then should it not apply to executives and their staff? Why should we in management, of all people, feel entitled to a carefree attitude? Those propagating a "culture of failure" seem to be living in a world in which there is neither professionalism nor due diligence. Liability and compensation appear not to bother them.

Hence: *Mistakes are not acceptable*. That must be the foundation. Taking this as given, it is possible to begin loosening the principle with due circumspection. When, where, by whom and under what circumstances may mistakes be made, what kind must not occur at all, and where might it be impossible to advance without making mistakes? My view is sometimes set against the claim that there are organizations in which staff are afraid to do anything, that people lie low – for fear of making mistakes. I will not only admit that there are such organizations, I am afraid that I have encountered them all too often in my practice as a consultant. It should be obvious that these are "sick" organizations and that there is a huge problem with *trust* in them. There are a number of factors that might encourage such a development, and grievous leadership errors in dealing with mistakes are among them.

CHALLENGES

We know that businesses *cannot* be wonderlands where happiness, wellness, and self-actualization are found. What is less clear is that they *ought not* to be. It is nonetheless surprising to find dreams of self-fulfillment turn up time and again even where one might least expect them: among people who like to think of themselves as especially performance-oriented and dynamic. They can be reliably identified by their habit of claiming always to "need new challenges."

Obliviousness or egomania?

Many candidates seem to think that being in search of challenges is a clear, important, and positive qualification for leadership tasks. In truth, however, this reveals nothing but their incompetence. In their cover letters, job applicants will often avow that they see the vacant position as an *urgent* "new challenge." High-profile appointees interviewed by the media will usually make reference to the tremendous challenges they look forward to addressing.

Sometimes, this may just be mindless chatter – embarrassing when captured on camera, and unacceptable in leaders who might be expected to think before speaking. Yet often enough, it may also hint at a deeper problem: that they are interested less in what the company's needs than their own. Their benchmark is not the task in hand, but their own requirements. Whether they are equal to the challenges they thirst for and are thus likely to produce results is of no concern to them.

The mixture of naïveté and arrogance may differ in each case, but in keeping with the times, they feel up to anything if only it is enough of a "challenge," as if some inward urge to test one's limits were some kind of qualification. They are in search of "kicks," preferably of the kind that the media might pay attention to. Alongside the visions that more often than not also afflict them, they usually leave their soon-to-be-appointed successors a pile of half-finished tasks or wreckage – while they are themselves off to confront new challenges. The story will ring as familiar in many of finance's hallowed corridors as it will in the world of start-ups.

A typical example is the figure of a top executive who, on the occasion of a surprisingly quick change of position, told a rapt television audience just this: that he was in need of ever-new challenges. Moreover, if he (in his own words) stopped having sweaty palms, he had lost interest in the job and it was time to move on. The effect of these words on some commentators was clear: They lapped up such phrases and thought them to be the epitome of modern management, all the while failing to notice that they were providing a platform for the dissemination of adolescent inanities and indeed the cloaking of a veritable disaster.

Out of one's depth

Might it not be conceivable that "sweaty palms" signal not extraordinary competence, but a manager hopelessly out his depth? What would you make of a pilot whose palms were sweating with the imminent challenge of an intercontinental flight? Or a surgeon before an operation? Would they not be better advised to keep practicing until such time as they were able to fulfill their tasks in a calm and composed manner – in a word, professionally?

"Beyond the limits," as the phrase goes, is all very well, but only for people who are capable of recognizing limits in the first place – and then put their minds, coolly and rationally, and with a clear understanding of the risks, think about how they might be surpassed. Even many of the best have regularly had to accept defeat. The achievements of Reinhold Messner, a mountaineer who exceeded what was thought possible not just once, but regularly, show above all how to avoid deadly risk rather than courting it and how to remain "within limits." His true strength lies not in his heroic courage, but in sober calculation and professional preparation.

In it for kicks – or for results?

There is nothing wrong with feeling challenged from time to time, as long is it not a euphemism for professional incompetence. I am all in favor of exploring the limits of one's abilities and pushing them back. But I do advise skepticism and careful scrutiny when people keep harping on the "challenges" they claim to need and seek. Nor is there any objection to be made to facing challenges and seeking out experiences – privately, that is, for instance doing extreme sports, on the racetrack, in a bivouac. Businesses, however, are run not for kicks, but for results. Their purpose is not to release adrenaline and set off nervous excitement. They exist in order to create utility for their customers from the strengths of their staff.

PERFORMANCE LIMITS

What can human beings accomplish? Where are their limits? The question remains unanswered to this day, and perhaps we will never know. But history proves that humans can achieve far more than was ever imagined in the past. The limits are always beyond where one might like to imagine them, conveniently close to one's own.

Yet the way people are raised, formed, and educated makes it hard to live by this insight. In some cases, artificial boundaries are deliberately imposed on people – to uphold the prevailing status quo, the relations of power and property. Other boundaries are drawn out of misguided hostility to excellence and a false sense of equality. That people have always proved their ability to overcome such resistance and break boundaries should give us confidence in the human potential for achievement.

In the very sphere that historically has exemplified an orientation towards achievement and performance – business – , however, more boundaries seem to be erected than pulled down nowadays. This is done not with the intention to cause harm, but because a few fundamentals of human development have fallen into neglect. They have been displaced by a fashionable, superficial humanism in training and qualification.

Artificial and altogether unnecessary boundaries are created by misleading doctrines of motivation. They are also set by widespread approaches to personal development that nearly always attack the problem from the wrong angle, by trying to eliminate weaknesses.

A first illustration may be found in motivational doctrines and the damage they cause in the training and further qualification of managers. It has become a ubiquitous and largely unquestioned truism that people will only work and perform if they are motivated. The next step follows logically: that people have a claim to being motivated. As long as this claim goes unmet, no performance is delivered: "I'm not feeling so hot today, boss, how about some motivation …?"

People have always worked, not because they fancied it, but because they had to or thought it their duty. Even in the developed countries, necessity is still an issue, albeit one largely tempered by the welfare system. This is a welcome development. Yet it has also spelled the decline of a sense of duty and obligation. Indeed, to insist on and appeal to duty is nearly certain to get one branded as hopelessly behind the times.

Testing boundaries

Anyone who will spring into action only when they care to do so and it seems agreeable – in other words, when motivated – will feel little inclination to explore their boundaries, let alone cross them when their motivation deserts them. To test boundaries is almost always an effort. It demands commitment and sometimes that final exertion that seems almost superhuman, but which time and time again has proved that humans can achieve more than others and they themselves might think possible.

This is most impressively on display in times of crisis, in the midst of war and disaster. What people in such situations are able to accomplish and to bear is almost beyond belief. But examples can be found in many other less exceptional situations: in science and the arts, in business and politics, in hospitals and families, in schools and churches.

Breaking boundaries

Seemingly fixed boundaries are crossed when people, rather than asking whether they are motivated, feel called to fulfill a task, take charge of a situation, and fulfill a duty. Nothing in such situations could be more risible, insignificant, or cynical than to ask after motivation, let alone pleasure.

The doctrine of motivation having taken root in so many minds, such an idea seems outmoded today. Yet it takes little analysis to conclude that no society could function if all people ever did was what they felt motivated to do. Instead of spreading motivational messages that turn out to be rather threadbare on inspection, it might be worth encouraging people to focus not on their motivation, but on their abilities.

A second example of unnecessary boundaries and people being discouraged from exploring them is found in the commonplace understanding of personality development. It is based chiefly on identifying weaknesses and trying to eliminate them.

Today, we have at our disposal the most sophisticated methods for identifying weaknesses and faults. And anyhow, people are highly skilled at finding fault in others. It is all too easy, therefore, to ignore that people are made successful not by eliminating their faults, but by developing their existing strengths and using them to the full.

The misguided but widespread and seemingly humane philosophy of addressing weaknesses does not offer a path to development. In fact, it hinders people rather than helping them, depriving them of the ability to discover their limits in the first place – never mind pushing them back. Eliminating one's weaknesses, which requires gargantuan exertions, seldom leads to more than mediocrity. At the end of this process, people arrive, physically or mentally exhausted, were other people started effortlessly. The effort is gigantic, the returns are poor.

All great achievements – in sports, the arts and sciences, business and politics – are the result of taking uncompromising advantage of pre-existing strengths. They are the accomplishments of people who encouraged themselves or were encouraged by others not to worry about their weaknesses and labor over their removal, but instead to make full use of their innate gifts.

MOTIVATION

There is nothing to be said against "motivation" as a term. What is dangerous, however, is the lack of leadership knowledge and ability that it tends to be associated with. For more than 70 years, motivation has been at the center of management training. If one asks executives what than most important task is, the answer is invariably: to motivate their staff.

Conversations about motivation soon reveal that knowledge of the topic is usually quite disjointed. Many managers have no clear idea of what the term means, and only few are familiar with the central theories. What if theories aren't even necessary? But why then should motivation be such a perennial issue?

The following suggestions might help us along the way: First off, a lot is to be gained simply by not demotivating people. This often happens when tasks are too piecemeal or unclear, when weaknesses and faults are harped on, when judiciously (and economically) applied praise is lacking, or when the elementary principles of fairness are neglected. Whether observing these warnings will automatically bring about motivation is less clear.

My second suggestion is to get over the idea that there will always be someone else, a third party, a boss, a superior, or someone else who will motivate you. Even allowing that this might generally be a viable idea, it is of no use to people in executive positions. If you hope one day to become a leader, a further step is necessary, the step from motivation to self-motivation. Waiting for someone else to motivate you is to defer your own accomplishments. To wait for external motivation is to be dependent, to be led, not a leader, even if coincidence or good fortune should raise you to higher positions.

To rely on others for motivation is to expose yourself to repeated and bitter disappointment, for there is no reason to assume that there will always be someone else to motivate you. Contrary to the prevalent notion of motivation, my advice is. "Learn to motivate yourself! Break your inner dependence on being motivated by others."

STRESS

The media are full of long stories about managers suffering from burnout. I take this problem very seriously because I know a number of people who are afflicted by it. Stress and overwork are still mentioned as the principal causes, although we now know the problem to be more complex.

There is no lack of therapies suggested for stressed-out managers. What is remarkable is that while many of them are interesting, none seems to be right. Is it conceivable that some of those concerning themselves with this problem are unfamiliar with how business works? Might it be that they compound this problem by basing their conclusions on the wrong people, which is to say managers who often suffer stress because they fail to cultivate their professionalism, but are all the more enthusiastic when it comes to chasing after the latest therapeutic fads?

Countless column inches are devoted to the umpteenth discussion of the phenomenon of stress and all its mental and physical consequences; and for the umpteenth time this discussion is one-sided, focusing only on negative stress, *dystress*, while ignoring the positive *eustress*. The opinions of experts are solicited, all of them leading lights of their discipline. The therapies they suggest are appealing: countless variations on regeneration, deep breathing, and letting go, coaching and empowerment, learning to listen and practicing empathy, networking, recreation etc. – and they may indeed help many sufferers.

But why are the simple things never mentioned? What about the following four suggestions: Professionalism in the fulfillment of tasks as the result of good training in management, a solid and methodical approach to work, a reasonably untroubled private life, and regular exercise? In more than 40 years of professional experience dealing with executives, I have never met anyone who suffered from debilitating stress in the presence of these four factors. Many of them work hard, quite frequently too much so; they may often find themselves in trouble, in a state of crisis, be worried or uncertain about their decisions; they are not always in a good mood, and they are often exhausted by the end of the working day ... What's so unusual about that? Do other people feel better? Are single mothers, surgeons, farmers, teachers, students in exams, nurses, waiters, salespeople, police officers, and truck drivers really better off?

Good managers, just like good doctors, judges, and football coaches, don't talk about themselves, they don't complain and they don't take their personal difficulties public. They concentrate on their tasks. They work to perfect their personal working methods. They have made the experience that it is possible constantly to improve and to take pleasure from it. They know that there is no limit to effectiveness and efficiency – save for those mental limits we set ourselves. Instead of excessive sensitivity, they are attentive to their time and mindful about using it. Their concern is with contents, not wrapping; with being rather than appearances. They waste no time on showmanship but instead cultivate craftsmanship; are interested in results not rituals, in output not input.

And above all: They have their tasks and obligations under control, they prioritize, and they see things through. This may leave them tired at the end of the day, but not stressed out. Effective working, time management, and finalizing tasks is how they win for themselves, their family and friends, and the good things in life – not always, but more often than one might think. There are two reasons why they don't give interviews about stress: because they don't have any and because they don't care to waste their time.

GENERATION X, Y, Z

I consider it dangerous in management to set too much store by particular ideas of human nature or classifications by type. Nearly every important topic in management, be it motivation, performance, satisfaction, values, or corporate culture, seems to be determined by a prior understanding of human nature. This makes it all the more importance to use such a concept with circumspection. Typecasting is dangerous because it can lead to rigid ideas about people when what is needed is flexibility.

Typecasting inevitably enters into a discussion that the American psychologist Douglas McGregor describes in *The Human Side of Enterprise* (1960), in which he introduces the concepts of "Theory X" and "Theory Y." These two ideas of human nature were ancient and hoary even then. They can be traced all the way back through the history of ideas. They are largely useless for management because their practical application does more harm than good.

One notion – Theory X – sees humans as weak and needy creatures, dependent on solidarity and community, incapable of taking charge of and responsibility for their lives, who find work painful, onerous, and thus to be avoided, who need to be motivated by others and are thus in need, as it were, of "redemption." The other – Theory Y – is the image of human beings as strong and capable, able to motivate themselves and taking pleasure in work, and who draw meaning and satisfaction from being in charge of their own destiny.

Such classifications live on in accounts of "Generation X" and "Generation Y" – and I for one am not sure whether "Generation Z" is supposed to refer to "Digital Natives" or "Millennials." After all, many Millennials are by no means "Digital Natives." Such compartmentalization is far from unambiguous.

Dispensing with labels

My advice is to do without an idea of human nature in management altogether and entirely. Not possible, it might be objected – after all, everyone has an idea of human nature ... True enough. We are never free of assumptions and opinions, but I suggest actively refusing to have an idea of human nature, because it courts the risk of falling prey to cliché and prejudice. This is – admittedly – no small task. But I am talking about managers and executives here, and a little effort in this respect does not seem too much to ask of them. We should begin by accepting that we simply do not know what people are like. No two are the same. All are unique individuals.

Do we even have to know what people are like? Managers are fortunately spared the problem of having to lead all people. They are merely confronted with the task of having to lead the eight, ten, or twelve individuals with whom fate, coincidence, or their own choice has brought them into a direct working relationship. That is why one needs only to know what these few people are like. At least *that* can be established.

Finding out what the individual is like

My point here is not to preach the virtue of being unprejudiced, desirable though it may be. My aim is a practical one. Refusing to accept a generalized view of human nature and admitting to not knowing what people are like leads to a key task: finding out what the individual with whom one has to work is like. I must emphasize: finding out, not making assumptions. It will soon easily become apparent that no one entirely conforms to a fixed idea, and especially not to a single one for life.

Imagine the colleague who clearly has nothing in mind but the end of the working day. Yet afterwards, she is highly dedicated and motivated in pursuit of her activity in a sports club, a charity, political party, or of a hobby or other special interest. In the office, she does only the bare minimum, but participates in every sponsored run. So what kind of person is she?

On the other hand, there is the colleague who performs very well at work, but is lackadaisical in his private life and spends his evenings browsing the web. What label to stick on him? Supposed X-types do not always display X-behavior, nor can Y-types be relied on to deliver Y-results. A person might go through phases of extreme productivity before hitting a rut for days or weeks, vegetating on the edge of depression. Plenty of people are down on Monday, on Tuesday they begin to feel more themselves, on Wednesday they might score an important success that boosts their motivation, on Thursday something goes wrong, and on Friday, let's face it, most people's minds are on the weekend. Under what category do these people fall? Some people are stupid in their youth and get wise with age, others take the opposite course. Most impressive are those far from rare people who unexpectedly excel themselves when they find their purpose, though nobody ever thought they would amount to much.

Every sports coach has learned not to typecast, but to consider each athlete's individual abilities and performance. To fixate on ideas of human nature not only runs the risk of doing an injustice to people and denying one's own capacity for change. It also means to neglect what is most important in management: to find out what individuals are capable of, what their strengths are – and to enable them to make their contribution.

IDENTIFICATION

Many companies ask their employees to identify with various things: With the firm, with its products, with their work, with the company's vision. That sounds plausible enough. In fact, it is widely held to express a particularly up-to-date corporate culture. I consider this wrong and am of the opinion that identification is neither necessary nor desirable. This unfashionable opinion is unlikely to win me many friends. Yet I believe it to be well founded.

Precise psychological term or sloppy language?

Closer scrutiny will usually reveal that – fortunately–"identification" is not used in its precise psychological sense. The term is rather taken to mean that staff should accept their company, its activities, and its products, and indeed should do so with some commitment and pride. I agree. One should indeed expect this and hence take measures to ensure that staff are able to muster this pride and commitment.

So is this a real problem or just a case of careless or unthinking language? As long as it does no harm, one need not be unduly worried. If, however, one takes "identification" to denote something anywhere close to the scientific, psychological meaning of the term, one is on a dangerous track. Psychologically speaking, identification denotes putting oneself in place of, equating oneself with another person or group, and taking on its motives and ideals as one's own. Is that really desirable? Should it even be desired?

Against this background, what is it supposed to mean when we are told to identify with a company's products, for example? 90 per cent of our national product consists of things like food, drink, clothing, consumer electronics, accelerator pedals, or garden hoses. How sick would a person have to be to identify, in the strict psychological sense, with mineral water, margarine, crackers, credit cards, or smartphones?

Is it not enough for a person, in his or her capacity as employee, to accept a product and to throw his or weight behind its development, production, or distribution? Staff, that much is true, must be convinced of a product's merits in order to sell it credibly. But to be convinced of something is not the same as identifying with it.

Pubescent symptoms

When do people identify with something or someone? For my part, when I was between 12 and 16 years old, I identified with the heroes of my time: with the pioneers of rock, with James Dean, John F. Kennedy, and the sports stars of the day, particularly in soccer and skiing. I pinned their photographs to my bedroom walls, and I would have walked to the ends of the earth to get their autographs. This neither was nor is unusual, but perfectly normal and healthy when you're 14. To put up life-sized posters and collect autographs at 34, however, to identify with heroes and idols in such a way, is quite another matter. What is a normal developmental stage in puberty is anything but 20 years later.

No connection with performance

Why should people identify with anything about the business or with the business itself? The literature on this topic has failed to produce any persuasive evidence that identification leads to better performance or anything else that might be important to a company.

Managers ought to enable people to deliver a performance important to the company and then give them the space to do so. More is not called for. We pay for the performance and not for the motivation or the feelings associated with it. Nor could we do so if we wanted to, because these sources must remain unknown to us. I would by no means deny that there could be reasons and motives that have a positive effect on a performance and its quality. But identification is not one of them. Far more important and more durable in in their effects than the somewhat shopworn concept of "identification" are terms like sense of duty, responsibility, dedication, conscientiousness, and thoroughness.

The most important thing is to give people the chance to recognize meaning in what they do. As Viktor Frankl, who is far less known in the theory and practice of management than the latter-day apostles of identification, said, after Nietzsche: "Knowing a *why* for living makes one tolerate nearly any *how*." And Frankl also makes the compelling case that no *how*, however attractive, will change matters for people unable any longer to see a *how*, a meaning.

The efforts of good, effective managers I directed at giving people tasks whose meaning they are able to recognize clearly – a task that is meaningful to them. Meaning – as Victor Frankl explains – is the decisive, most durable and effective motivator, compared with which all others pale in significance.[4]

Loss of Objectivity

A final thought, and perhaps the most important with respect to leadership: Identification, in the psychological sense, is as a rule connected to the loss of the ability to think critically and make considered judgments. Identifying with someone or something entails a loss of distance from the object of identification. In doing so, a person loses the crucial precondition for reaching objective judgments. But that, even when it is difficult, is what we should expect from leaders: enough distance to think clearly and judge soundly. There can be no absolute and final objectivity, but we are able to create conditions that enable a lesser or greater degree of objectivity. As an executive I would prefer to be surrounded by colleagues and staff who are able to say, "Things aren't going right here, we need to make changes."

This is beyond the abilities of people who identify. They become yes-men, easily led and agreeable company, but no longer any help. Such people agree with everything, they may even be enthusiastic in their identification, but they are no leaders and may even be dangerous.

TALENT

One of the great confidence tricks to sweep human resources departments was inaugurated when the "war for talent" was declared. If the martial image was not enough to set alarm bells ringing, at least the term should have been "war for performance." But by now, HR people seem unable to get through a presentation without referring to "talent." As if business were some TV reality show, the search is on for "talented people, indeed the "super" or "mega" talented will do. If asked what they mean, most HR people will reply vaguely: "Some kind of special gift ... somebody who's just really good."

I would thus recommend that we dispense with the word "talent" if at all possible. As is so often the case in contemporary management teaching, it directs attention towards the rare, the particular, the exceptional. The Cambridge Dictionary defines "talent" as "a natural ability to be good at something, especially without being taught," Merriam-Webster as "a special often athletic, creative, or artistic aptitude." No doubt some people are endowed with such gifts. Yet they are not of decisive importance for management and an organization's success. Talent is not what counts in management – results are. Everyone knows people who might reasonably be describes as "talented," yet have failed ever to make anything much of it. As familiar is the opposite: people who seem to lack any notable gift, yet can claim remarkable achievements. If one must use the word, the focus should be on the *uses* to which talent is put – for what counts is not talent alone, but what one makes of it.

What we need is an awareness of an individual's specific strengths. Strengths are not the same as talent. They are more down-to-earth, specific, and practical. The preachers of talent tend to make an about-turn at this point and claim to mean the same thing by "talent" as I do by "strengths." But that is a confusion analogous to that between possession and ownership, or mass and density. It is playing fast and loose with terminology at the cost of clarity and precision.

POTENTIAL

A word that belongs in the same category as "talent" and is often used synonymously is "potential," particularly when amplified to the popular "high potential," meaning "a promising individual." My advice is to look not at potential, but at *performance*, and to value high performance, not "high potential."

These are not one and the same thing. Potential is possibility, a promise – a promise all too often revealed to have been empty; something for which one might hope, but without any guarantee of fulfillment. Performance, on the other hand, *is* the proof, its own evidence, something to build on. We do not have the means to gauge potential accurately. All that we can reliably measure are the performance somebody delivers and the strengths evident therein. Everything else is conjecture, hope, projection. All we can do is to infer future performance from previous performance, though such conclusions are not perforce reliable. Nonetheless, performance already delivered must be at the center of attention, not some nebulous potential. When a position is to be filled, the choice should not be from among "potentials," but a list of "performers."

Well-run organizations do not rely on potential. They may use the word, but will take care of how, of what is meant. Only real performance (not assessments) and real-life tests can provide a basis on which to predict potential. Another point is decisive: Both terms – talent and potential – divert attention to the individual alone, as if the individual contained the key to success. Doing so overlooks that two elements are important for efficacy and success. One is people and their specific strengths, the other is the specific task that is to be performed. I do not mean a job or a position, but a specific task, an assignment. An assignment is distinct from the position itself: It is the decisive, key priority to be addressed by the holder of a position in the foreseeable future.

If one wishes to foster performance in people and produce results for the organization, people's strengths must be made to be congruent with the tasks. Admittedly, this is not an easy operation, but it is far from impossible. The lever is to change tasks, not people. Fixating on talent and potential leads one to forget the second element, the task. Well-run organizations focus on tasks. In doing so, they achieve remarkable successes with ordinary people, who are capable of extraordinary achievements if their strengths are brought into harmony with their tasks.

PRAISE

One of the strongest motivating factors is praise. This statement seems to require little explanation and meet with broad approval. Precisely there lies the danger of overusing praise. Praise can serve to motivate only under very specific conditions, namely, when it is serious and given by a person of respect.

That is why I think it wrong to praise daily. Praise is not just the strongest motivating factor, but the one to wear out the soonest from ill-use. Not everybody, but most people have a keen sense for when they are being praised deservedly or otherwise. We all know that we don't put in a praiseworthy performance every day, and we also know that a workaday job is not deserving of any special praise. Even schoolchildren are already aware of that.

A superior who makes inflated to use of praise is likely to be perceived as manipulative, the praise itself as a tool of conditioning. And nothing is more humiliating than to be the object of conditioning. There is but one correct maxim: *Be economical with praise! And do not praise what goes without saying, but the exceptional performance!* On the whole, people do not expect praise for the everyday performance they have contractually undertaken to deliver and for which they are paid. Admittedly, a positive word from time to time is welcome. But only few will find the absence of such a kind word to be a real problem. Praise is appropriate and necessary for truly exceptional performances, for that which people do over and above their obligations, and for achieving special success.

However, there is another type of person, people who actually *do* need praise every day, but lack any sense of whether they deserve to be singled out for recognition or not. But such people must not the allowed to set the standard for an organization; rather, they are a serious problem. Ultimately, they make leadership and performance impossible, they put a strain on working relations, they are a problem for everyone else – a problem especially where the fair treatment of people is concerned. In essence, they represent a constant, personified demand for privileged treatment. No team, no organization can tolerate this in the long run. That is why such workers should not be the benchmark. The strongest motivating factor can lose its power in no time at all, and the infantilization of the organization is the consequence.

HIERARCHY

The word "hierarchy" seems to have become relegated to the sphere of power and the abuse of power, of command and obedience, of domination and submission. This is the realm of all that is negative, obsolete, rigid, and immobile. Yet hierarchy is the oldest and most durable principle of organization – in hunting packs, tribes and clans, farms and royal courts, churches and armies. Where are the exceptions?

Not only in business has the lesson been learned that solitary decisions made at the top of a hierarchy can be disastrous. Hierarchies, *on the one hand*, are prone to abuses of power and corruption in the interest of its preservation. *On the other hand*, hierarchies led by truly competent people, endowed with far-reaching powers of decision, may be responsible for some of greatest deeds and most revered achievements – in architecture, art, and music, in politics, business, and science.

On closer consideration, there is no necessary *functional* connection between hierarchy on the one hand and participation, flexibility, adaptability, and speed of action on the other. It entirely possible for hierarchically structured organizations to be led at eye level, with an emphasis on participation – or the reverse. Hierarchic organizations can be sites of freedom or of oppression, they can be both simultaneously and much more still.

Consider the air traffic controller in charge of take-off and landing at an airport. She is not the superior of the pilots she guides and coordinates. Yet in specified situations, hers is the sole decisive authority, the one-person responsibility. Air traffic controllers guide about 1 500 aircraft movements daily at Frankfurt Airport alone – some 200,000 worldwide. They ensure the safety of the skies under all imaginable conditions. But the hierarchic, disciplinary path is embodied not in them, but in the flight captains.

One point responsibility can, however, also be assigned to a body of people. This may be done by law, as in the case of the executive and supervisory boards that German law stipulates for listed companies, or by charter or statue, as is typically the case with advisory boards, which any organization can summon.

An important principle that enables hierarchies to function is that of *redundancy of potential command*, which maintains that "power resides where information resides," as the neurophysiologist and cybernetician Warren McCulloch put it in 1965. It signifies that power is *not* necessarily founded in a system's hierarchy, though it may have *a* power. "Command" is located wherever the situationally optimum information converges. The networks of neurons provide a physiological example of this functional principle.

There's no boss in the brain – but there are rules

Our brain is governed by rules, but not by a "boss." Yet there are hierarchical functional structures that exercise the power of command, specifically the constantly changing neuronal networks that possess the *most relevant in-*

formation in any given moment. In soccer, *power and control* are situated wherever the ball is. On the meta level of the game's regulation, power and control are vested in the referee who, in turn, is *not* the players' boss. This is an up-to-date idea: doing away not with hierarchies as such, but with *rigid* hierarchies. And it works. Tasks, decisions, competences, and responsibilities are shifted to the point at which – irrespective of established, traditional, or even "inherited" hierarchies – the knowledge of the situation and its demands is the greatest. A system may be endowed with functionalities that it would not otherwise possess; one can "let a system run itself" by deliberately doing nothing, and by the same means – including non-intervention – dysfunction may be triggered. The manner in which hierarchy is handled may have positive or negative consequences.

Responsibility is the only tenable legitimation

The time of rigid hierarchy is at an end. New forms of systems are emerging – not a hierarchy of power, but a hierarchy of systems, which are embedded in one another recursively. Management will thus be more efficacious, not less, and moreover without having to deploy power, because self-regulation develops. In the language of systems theory and cybernetics, one might say that a functioning organization must be constructed recursively, that the parts contain the whole and represent it. In physics, specifically in chaos theory, talk would be of fractals. The principle of recursion is one of the most important architectural and functional patterns in nature and its evolution. However an organization may be designed, it is in need of an authority able to speak the last word and bring about a decision. This authority may be vested in individuals as well as in committees. The practice of effective management is not about hierarchy as power personified. The functionality of hierarchy is *responsibility*. It is hierarchy's sole tenable legitimation.

PARTICIPATION

Effective participation in organizations is something other than democracy in society, and its goals and objectives are different. Participation is an essential functional principle for right and good management and beyond that for true leadership. It is based, however, not on equality, as is the case in democracy, but on the principles of efficacious functioning, effective communication, and right thinking and action. Yet media and literature currently tend to promote the democratic account of participation. What matters for organizations is thus easily overlooked.

No end in itself

Today, participation is already among the most important functional principles of organization. And this importance is set to increase for the organizations of the future. There will probably be far more varieties and forms participation than today. And these new forms of participation will also fulfill certain, perhaps even many different purposes, which already make real participation indispensable to functioning organizations today.

But participation is not an end in itself. Piping up for the sake of talking, participating for its own sake, will be a thing of the past. Surely so will be participation to the end of giving people the mere "feeling" of having a say in the way things are run. Participation thus understood is obsolete. Having a say must be taken seriously on both sides. A "feeling" is not enough.

The principal aim of participation in organizations is clear: to make responsibility an integral part of the task. Commercial enterprises are not run on democratic principles, and the same is true for most other organizations in society. It is also true, and indeed particularly so, of institutions created in order actively to maintain a democratic social order, for instance political parties, ministries, trade unions, security forces, and the judiciary.

The way a society is ordered is not the same as the order of its organizations. That we organize a society and the state along to democratic lines has little to say about the optimum form of other kinds of organization. This often gives rise to confusion and can be harmful to state and society as well as to their organizations. Participation is indispensable *to functioning organizations* for the three following reasons, though more might be adduced:

To interconnect knowledge, amplify intelligence, and for better decisions

First, in order to make the organization of knowledge in our knowledge society intelligent, for the purpose of interconnecting the knowledge of so many people that the result is the emergence and amplification of intelligence. To use all the information needed for better decisions and to ensure their optimal implementation. This is participation not as a right, but as an obligation. In nearly all comments on decision-making processes, there is a more or less implicit question concerning the *involvement of those directly affected*, that is to say, about participatory, even democratic processes. There are at least *two* aspects to this question about participation in decision-making processes:

The first case is a decision for which, whether by law or by statute, not a person but a committee is responsible, for instance a board of directors, with clear rules set for the *participation* of its members. Normally in such, the appropriate rules will also make provision for how to deal with disagreement among members, for the proportion of votes needed to pass a decision in the absence of unanimity. But unanimity should be the goal when really important decisions are at stake, irrespective of the formal rules. Of course it can take rather log to reach a consensus. Yet many people are not sufficiently aware that *a viable consensus can only be reached by an open discussion of dissenting opinions*.

The second case concerns a general question of worker participation in an organization, particularly that of members of staff who are involved in the implementation of the decision and/or those affected by the decisions consequences.

Participatory decision-making and, more generally, participatory leadership are among the most talked-about topics of recent decades. A considerable, if not the overwhelming part of this discussion is ideologically weighted and thus misguided. Experience has shown that hurriedly implementing participation in management as an end in itself leads to the very opposite of the effects desired of true participation.

For the emergence of meta-information

Second, participation in organizations is important in order to go from information to meta-information. This is indispensable if an organization is to be brought to the state ("operating mode") of preparedness for critical situations: Situations in which a large number of people must act in a manner that is fast, coordinated, targeted, and largely error-free. Quite generally, to make coordinated action on the part of many people possible in the first place. Here, participation is a right as well as a duty. Information and communication are the way to lead systems – including social systems and teams. In doing so, people are enabled to guide themselves. However, in complex situations it is not enough to inform staff in the usual sense, but rather to inform them in such a way as to allow collective information to emerge, to ensure that all are informed to an equal degree – and know it. And all must be made aware of what that information substantially means.

Meta-communication means communication about communication. It means transmitting knowledge in such a way as to ensure that everyone knows that everyone knows everything necessary to completing a task or acting in a particular situation. Only then are people and teams in a position to guide themselves and, if needed, to re-organize themselves, and not just as individuals, but as teams and particularly as large collectives. This kind of meta-communication is carried to great perfection – i.e. functional reliability – in emergency services, air crews, air traffic control centers, and the like. It must be ensured that everyone knows exactly what to do in an emergency. This kind of communication will rapidly spread to most other kinds of organization – indeed it will *have to*, if functional reliability is required in highly complex situations. It will become increasingly important not just to talk to one another, but to communicate effectively, which is not the same.

For effective learning

The third reason why participation is essential in and for organizations is its importance for effective learning. To develop and enable managers – not just young ones, but of all ages – as fully rounded human beings, participation will only grow in importance. Participation is one of the most important paths to genuine learning – participation in real time, in real life. This is where participation becomes an individual's right and an organization's obligation.

TEAMWORK

For a long time and almost without exception, management viewed teamwork in a thoroughly positive light: Teamwork was regarded as not just one *possible* way of working, but as the *only one desirable*. Teams are fundamentally and generally held to be superior to individuals. Teams are viewed as inherently innovative, creative, and "better" than the individual. And yet the average "team" in an organization is usually nothing of the kind, but merely a group of people who somehow – for better or for worse – have to work together. An exception is the kind of team often called on to troubleshoot throughout an organization.

The need for teams is an ancient one, and working together is among the foundations of our sociability. But does it follow *dogmatically* that the team is the *only worthwhile working unit*? Does every social interaction already constitute teamwork? The distinction between communication, coordination, cooperation, and collaboration is underdeveloped. All these processes *can* take place within a team. The reverse is not necessarily the case.

What's so hard about teamwork?

Since the dawn of humanity, working together has been a natural part of everyday life. What we now call a team is the foundation of any kind of social order. We are look-

90

ing at what might be called the constitutive element of society, people cooperating in various form to deal with the challenges of each sphere of life, from the family in its various forms and prehistoric bands of hunters to the communities of the farm, the workshop, the village. No one could have survived without cooperation. The figure of Robinson Crusoe is so striking because of its improbability.

For this reason, nobody ever had a problem with working as part of a team with others. To do so needed to be neither learned nor taught. Life as such took place in teams. Life was teamwork. Which is why teamwork and so-called social skills are never explicitly discussed by historians. At any rate, I have yet to come across a phrase like: "… and then the ancient Egyptians invented teamwork."

So what happened to make the most commonplace and unquestioned habit of millennia suddenly seem so important and difficult that it requires special training and has become a criterion deciding not just the fate of one's career, but an individual's professional usefulness altogether? Why is today's received wisdom that everything *must* be done in a team? Are our organizations really so full of people who never learned to complete a task themselves? Or do many people just find it convenient to take cover in a working group?

What certainly has changed are the speed, dynamic, and complexity of today's communication, cooperation, coordination, and collaboration. What has thus often increased are *nonsensical forms of organization* and impractical approaches to the division of labor. Anyone who has had to work, for instance, in a matrix organization – which tend to be introduced far too quickly, with far too little thought – needs an excess of team skills to a degree seldom encountered. No seminar is able to make up for shortfalls of that order. A matrix organization can work perfectly – if it happens to be staffed by saints. Most of us have to work within all too human limitations, which is why it is better to change the organization, not the people.

The purpose of an organization is not to make life hard for people. On the contrary, it is meant to make working easier. Once people no longer have to struggle against performance-inhibiting organizations, it turns out that most of them can work quite well together without much difficulty. And that is because working together is among the normal skills of perfectly average people.

Nobody would come up with the inane idea to make people drive a car, or play chess or a musical instrument, in a team. It is clear to all that many *tasks of this kind* can be performed only by individuals if there is to be any prospect of success and efficiency, let alone brilliance. No amount of teambuilding would produce even mediocre results. It is one thing to say that performing a symphony is a team exercise. Every musician is aware of that. It does not follow that it takes a team to blow a trumpet.

If management were to *design positions and tasks* with the same *care* that a composer uses when scoring the individual parts of a symphony, teamwork would not be an issue, or rather: One could count on ordinary people already being in possession of the skills needed to work together. Teamwork wouldn't be an issue. And the opposite? No amount of training will make up for errors in the design of positions and tasks, or in the set-up of the organization. What it takes for people to work together may thus be largely assumed – *if the circumstances are well designed*.

Unnecessary idealization and genuine performance

And what about excellent performance? Is the truly superlative achievement, the great creative inspiration, a matter solely for the team? Are the innate team skills of ordinary people still enough? Or is this where special training in organizations comes in?

Nearly all great achievements, especially those we think of as breakthroughs, were the achievements of individuals – sometimes supported by others, but hardly ever as part of a team. That is true of all the arts: Team compositions in music are as rare as great works of literature written in teams; and while paintings and sculptures may have been created in workshops, they are truly the work of an individual mind.

Teams are tools, as is solitary work. Neither form should be ignored or overpraised. How to work, what is the best format for a job, must be determined with reference to *the task in hand, not dogma*. In the world of organizations, tasks must be designed so as to be within the power of ordinary people (there are no others) with ordinary skills (no others can be learned) to fulfill. *Organizations that want to achieve results must be capable of both teamwork and individual performance*. What counts is the *efficacy* in relation to the set tasks. We thus need both: effective individual work and efficacious team-work. As always in management, efficacy decides how the right things are to be done.

TOP MANAGEMENT TEAMS

The work of top management is teamwork of the most exacting kind. Contrary to fashionable opinion, well-functioning executive top management teams are held together not by "culture" or the similarly nebulous "chemistry." The secret of effective top-level teams is adherence to principles and rules agreed on in advance. Wherever the failure of such teams is examined, it turns out that a crucial and frequent reason is to be found in ignorance or defiance of this fact.

Three principles

The first principle is that the tasks of the executive team must be clearly defined. A top management team is the place neither for self-actualization nor, as some would have it, for a discourse of democratic consensus-building. Teams are needed where the tasks to be fulfilled exceed the power and abilities of individuals. In other cases, we can spare ourselves the complications typically associated with teams. To demand clarity of tasks may seem banal or superfluous. Yet the fact is that this demand is all too seldom met.

The second rule is that effective teams must have a well-thought-out division of labor. Tasks are fulfilled in coordination, but not by a group effort as such. Everyone does their part of the task; all others know what that is and must be able to rely on it. For that reason, good teams possess well-considered and precisely phrased rules that define who is responsible for what.

The third principle allowing top-level teams to work is the most concise: strict discipline. Lack of discipline poisons any kind of team, not just in management and not just at the head of an organization. However, that is where the absence of discipline can wreak the most havoc. Elements of discipline include forgoing vanities and cults of personality, and extend to personal goals being curbed in favor of the organization's. If there is no conflict between these goals – so much the better. But anyone using a business or organization as vehicle for their personal ambitions represents a serious risk.

Six rules

Besides these three principles, well-functioning top-level teams observe the following six following rules:

First, each member of a top management team has the last word in his or her sphere of responsibility, and speaks *bindingly* for the team as a whole.

Second, nobody is to decide outside his or her own sphere of responsibility. These two rules are mutually re-enforcing. They create clarity and speed, and they ensure the capacity for action. To violate these two rules not only leads to hopeless confusion, paralyzing an organization's effectiveness, but invariably causes power struggles.

Third: Certain decisions must be reserved for the team as a whole. This rule is an insurance against abuse of the first two, which, but for this corrective, might promote the development of fiefdoms within an organization – and sooner or later spell the team's downfall. Speed and ability to act are important, but must serve the whole. Certain decisions thus require the agreement of all. Typical cases include major acquisitions, entering into alliances, critical innovations, and sensitive personnel matters.

Fourth, there must be no qualification of team members by other team members outside the team. A team's members needn't like each other. But there must be no agitation of any kind. This rule applies on the outside. Within a team, there may be intense conflict. That is hardly to be avoided where essential and risky decisions with respect to the whole are at stake. But outwardly, one must express no opinions about one's colleagues. Even to praise them would be an inappropriate qualification.

Fifth: Each member of the team is obliged to keep all others informed about what is going on within the sphere of his or her responsibility. This, too, is a corrective to rule one. If full autonomous powers of decision-making are granted in each sphere, then the guarantee of full transparency must be the corollary.

Sixth: Contrary to widespread opinion, a well-functioning top team is not a group of equals, though the statutes may proclaim otherwise. Teams are not about democracy, but about effectiveness. Each member is part of the team in order to make a certain contribution. Hence, good teams are structured, and what is more, they are led. The principal and foremost task of a team leader in top management, whatever the official title may be, is to ensure strict adherence to the rules.

If these rules and principles are adhered to, the much-vaunted "chemistry" is largely irrelevant. If it works, so much the better; if not, we still have a functioning team – not on account of the chemistry, but the rules. No reasonable person should put an organization at the mercy of accidents of chemistry.

PERSONNEL DECISIONS

Successful leadership of a business rests on two pillars: setting a good personal example and making the right personnel decisions. Both are indispensable, and both brook no compromise. Personnel decisions are the ultimate means of leading an organization. They do not require any particular ingenuity, though many may find such skill and artfulness fascinating. This is the hallmark of the dilettante. What is needed are conscientiousness and rigorous adherence to a few principles.

The first principle is: *Nobody has an intuitive grasp of human nature*. Although many would baulk at this statement, truly experienced people do not rely on intuition – least of all those who are actually highly experienced in making personnel decisions. Intuition and first impressions give bad advice. The risk involved in making personnel decisions is too great to be left to gut feeling.

The second principle is: *Nobody is an all-round genius*. Especially when looking to fill high positions, one is apt to fall into the trap of looking for an all-round genius, a man for all seasons, a Renaissance man, or polymath – call it what you will.

Such a figure is entirely fictitious, though its various iterations take center stage in any number of hokey management doctrines. It is possible to describe this figure but never to find it. Knowing this, many decision-makers fall into the opposite trap: They choose the people with the fewest faults, they go for the "well-rounded personality." Whereas the one error keeps one looking for the impossible, the other leads straight to the trap of mediocrity. The secret of an organization's success lies neither in Renaissance men nor in well-rounded personalities. It lies in finding people whose strengths are the ones a business needs to succeed in its particular situation.

The third principle is: *Whoever makes wrong decisions must bear the responsibility for them and correct them*. For every failure there is someone who put him in that place. It is this someone, not the person hired, who should be responsibility for rectifying the bad decision. The famous "Peter principle," which holds that "managers rise to the level of their incompetence," is well observed, but not a law of nature. It must not be used as an excuse for negligence.

The fourth principle is: *The quick personnel decision is almost always a bad decision*. Considering the importance of such decisions, their long-term character, and the signals they send out across the organization, personnel decisions at the highest level must always be made exercising all conceivable and humanly possible diligence, care, and thoroughness. This takes time – time that must be taken.

The fifth principle is: *Never place a new person in a function that is new and critical to the organization*. New and important tasks must be entrusted only in people whom one already knows and of whose character and abilities one thus can have a reasonably accurate idea based on experience. Unknown people must be given known tasks. To depart from this principle is to set up an equation containing to unknown variables and thus to take an incalculable risk. Generally speaking, it is possible to abide by this principle.

What to do when treasures become burdens?

This fifth principle often meets its limits in times of the Great Transformation and of fundamental change – not only when top-level positions need to be filled from outside. For the tasks in ever more areas, of which digitalization is but one, are so new that they can be entrusted only too new people. Personnel decisions for paths not yet beaten are among the hardest.

In processes of substitution, virtually all previous navigational aids are not only rendered obsolete, but they point – and quite persuasively – in the wrong direction. Experience once so valuable and treasured suddenly becomes the greatest obstacle in the way of changing from a previous activity to a completely new one: that of innovation. All the best know-how with regard to the tried and tested can become a heavy burden when what is needed is to steer a new course. Quite suddenly, the *best people* cease to be the *right* ones.

So who are the "right people"? The question is hard enough to answer in personnel decisions within today's familiar business. But are the right people for *tomorrow's business*? And, harder still, who are the people who can master the *transition*? Who are the people who can cope with the unforeseeable, with a system that is neither known nor can be known? How do they work under such conditions – and manage, moreover, to be effective?

The most important step in the decision-making process is to think through the principal task posed by the vacant position thoroughly and conscientiously in the light of a particular question. The point is not to create one of the usual search profiles. Not "what demands does this position make?" should be the key question, but *"what specific task does the occupant of this position face in the foreseeable future?"* Or: *"What concrete assignment will have to be fulfilled?"* This distinction between *job* (or *position*) and *task* (or *assignment*) is all too often overlooked.

It is not too difficult to describe the job of a COO, a board member, or a head of IT or marketing in general terms. What is far more difficult is to define the concrete task associated with this position with sufficient accuracy. That, and not the job profile, must be the dominant criterion. A position may be called "managing director," but will the assignment be to continue to lead a thriving business? Or is the task to accomplish a turnaround? Will the business be able to grow on its own resources or will it need to push ahead with a takeover strategy? Will strategic alliances need to be forged? Will the organization's transition have to be managed?

It is rare that one and the same person is able to fulfill each of these assignments equally well. This leads to the question what specific strengths the fulfillment of the key task requires, for instance with regard to expertise, experience, and personality. Here especially, one should look not for the "all-round good person," but for the strengths a person brings specifically to the tasks assigned. Weaknesses that might be discovered – and more easily than strengths, as it happens – naturally reduce someone's chances of being picked, but it is for strengths that a successful candidate should ultimately be hired.

VISION

One should be wary of the subtle differences in meaning between identical-sounding words across languages. "Vision" is one such case. Until the early 1990s, the standard German dictionary defined "vision" as a "sensory illusion," an "optical hallucination," or a "supernatural apparition as a religious experience." And that, indeed, was what the word denoted to German-speakers for hundreds of years. Only quite recently was a meaning added that approaches its primary English connotation and makes the word useful for management: "somebody's imagining, especially an image drawn with reference to the future."

This convergence of the German with the English to denote a "design for the future" is a distinct improvement as far as management is concerned. Today's "visions" tend to be rather more substantial. Yet the old meaning dies hard, and with it the temptation to dignify by the epithet "vision" vague yet elaborate and flowery phrases containing scant information and thus carrying little force of conviction.

Visions, good & bad

One hazard remains: the inability to distinguish bad visions from good. The literature on vision offers no advice on how to tell one apart from the other, how to sift viable concepts from nonsense, and what the difference might be between wishful thinking and useable ideas.

Not only are criteria missing, the problem is not even discussed. When I once asked one of the most prolific authors of vision books how she thought the wheat could be separated from the chaff, she not only found herself unable to give me an answer, but took offense at my question. From time to time, one must accept offense where one would have hoped for an informed opinion and leave it at that, but that is no solution to the problem. In another, in which I asked a professor at a respected university for a definition, he gleefully replied: "A vision is a dream with a deadline." A good way to start a presentation, no doubt, but not a useful definition for serious work. Every dream must come to an end, and nightmares, too – thank goodness.

Mission

That is why I prefer more substantial and down-to-earth terms. "Guiding principle" is one, and "business mission" better still. I am aware that both have their drawbacks and blind spots, but anyone with a solid training in management who is familiar with the appropriate literature will know what they mean. The key is to look for content and substance, not the fancy semantic wrapping.

Imagination and bold ideas are important elements of good leadership. But a clear distinction must be drawn between good and bad, useful and useless ideas. A vision in this sense can, however, be a good beginning to finding and framing a mission for an organization. Unfortunately, both vision and mission continue to be used as slogans in marketing and advertising, although they can and ought to be so much more. To make them so, Peter F. Drucker laid a solid foundation in his *Theory of the Business*. Drucker postulates three questions to help formulate a meaningful and forward-looking mission. First, *what are the requirements of the market or of society?* Second, *what are the business's strengths?* And third, *what do we believe in?* To answer these searching questions conscientiously is a major and usually hard task for top management.

I have expanded these elements to encompass the relations in which they are situated. Customer value emerges from the interaction between demand and strengths. A company's strengths and the convictions of its workforce produce the cultural values of pride, self-respect, and self-confidence. Finally, purpose, which is so important, is created between the workforce and the market's needs. To find and frame a mission with these elements may begin with a vision statement, but must not stop there. If the mission is clear, one can still try to derive a catchy slogan from it.

EMOTIONS

One can expect general agreement for demanding more "gut" and less "head." Appeals for more emotion in management, in their manifold guises, do well in the marketplace. Conversely, one can be sure of meeting with bitter hostility for making the opposite call, for less "gut" and more "head." Even to suggest a balance between the two is often enough greeted with suspicion. The quality of these discussions is abysmal, their dogmatism medieval.

Emotions are part of human nature and hence of the organizations in which humans work; they are one and perhaps the most important functional component, as the social sciences and the highly revealing findings of behavioral economics have taught us.[5] This should be known and put to good use. But feelings themselves are no help in understanding such systems and situations, and to act correctly within them. One of the crucial obstacles is that feeling of subjective certainty that emotions, as a rule, entail.

Only positive emotions?

When the talk is of emotions and their beneficial effects in management, the implicit reference is to positive emotions, good feelings: pleasure, trust, humanity, compassion, empathy, sympathy. Who would want to miss them? But are there not others? There is barely a word on negative, destructive, bad feelings. Yet do envy, hatred, jealousy, resentment, and aggression not also exist? Are they what we want to bring to our organizations when we call for more "gut"? Clearly, it is not enough just to demand more emotion. The path to culture and civilization follows humanity having learned to curb its emotions, instincts, and drives, to discipline them.[6] Many emotions are socially highly destructive in character. To discipline such destructive emotions is the main purpose of manners, morals, law, and custom.

Humans are social animals only to the extent that they have learned to follow rules rather than surrender to their impulses. They are human not because they have emotions, but on the contrary, because they have their emotions under control.

For this reason, it is advisable to replace emotion with correctness in organizations – if they are to function. In my over thirty years of day-to-day work with managers, every conflict was either rooted in emotion or exacerbated by it. Things may look different in our personal lives. Yet in an organization, emotions – sometimes even positive ones – often spell trouble.

Emotion does not make up for poor thinking

We all know that the human intellect is prone to error. Why feelings should not suffer from this defect all too often remains unexplained. Yet notwithstanding all arguments and evidence to the contrary, the mere unsupported claim that feelings are somehow superior to the intellect exhibits remarkable tenacity. And though evidence may still not be forthcoming, one can at least keep repeating the claim – with added emotion, of course.

There seems to be no shame in setting emotion above reason and thinking. Feeling is associated with warmth and humanity, intellect with their opposite, with coldness, and if not exactly with inhumanity, then at any rate with "icy" calculation. This stark dichotomy, which is set up over and again, is dangerous and wrong. It is wrong not least because the logical opposite of rational is not emotional, but irrational, and that of emotional unemotional, non-emotional or unfeeling.

The ubiquity of emotion and its strong effect should not mislead us as to its reliability as an aid to orientation and navigation. Feelings are situated in what, evolutionarily speaking, is a very old part of the brain, the so-called limbic system. They may have been dependable under the circumstances of their development. But is that still the case now, in an environment that has changed beyond recognition?[7] Might it not be that they are in fact highly unreliable? So unreliable that the only organisms to have developed further are those whose evolution, adapting to the growing complexity of their surroundings, developed a cerebrum with the capacity for thought and reason – one that can correct the limbic system's defects and extend the brain's abilities?

This is to deny neither the existence of emotions nor their importance. It is also true that feats of reasoning take place in the context of emotion, and that thought processes are accompanied by feelings. There is no such thing as pure reason, and the philosophy of strict rationalism that pretended otherwise has been immensely harmful. Yet I find it no less harmful – and indeed grossly negligent – to recommend that emotions should always be given free rein in management, that managers should rely on their feelings.

GUT DECISIONS

Head or gut? Intelligence or intuition? Thinking or feeling? Many people trust their "gut feeling" to make better, more reliable decisions than their brain. In private life, that is all very well – each to his own. But managers, too, are often advised to trust obscure intuitions rather than well thought-out decisions. A whole industry of seminars, coaches, books, and media promotes this idea. As proof of the importance of gut instinct and intuition (and are they really identical?), surveys are often cited, according to which a majority of managers claim to make their decisions based on gut feeling.

Leaving aside the considerable margin of error in decisions based on feeling alone – for the choice of life partner, check the divorce statistics; for investment choices, see the history of market bubbles or individual bank balances – a few simple tests will suffice to expose the shortcomings of such judgment calls.

Outside climate-controlled spaces, only few people are capable of accurately estimating the temperature. Subjective perceptions of warm or cold may bear little resemblance to thermometer readings. Similarly with time: one's sense of time is often hopelessly askew and dependent on circumstance. 10 minutes in the dentist's chair can feel like an eternity, whereas two hours of watching an exciting game will pass in a flash. For the realm of complex systems, Jay Forrester, in his path-breaking studies at MIT, has shown that complex systems are *counterintuitive*: to grasp and comprehend them, let alone predict their behavior, based on feeling alone is a risky business. Trying to predict the weather intuitively in temperate climates will soon confirm this assessment.

Head or gut?

It is remarkable that no scientific study has yet been able to prove the superiority of the gut over the head in those points that matter the matter the most to top management. What is at stake there are far-reaching, risky, and above all complex decisions. Above all, what counts is making right decisions.

For all the shortcomings to which the human intellect is generally prone, there is still no persuasive evidence that emotion might be able to replace it – certainly not where understanding complex systems, their management, and the decision-making they require are concerned. It is also worth noting that Wolf Singer, Germany's most eminent neuroscientist, has plainly stated: "We have no intuition for complexity." What we owe modern research into intuition is above all support for the long-established insight that human decisions are not governed by the limited, unrealistic, economic rationality so beloved of the discipline of economics, and particularly that of management studies. Management, and more still leadership, begin only where purely economic rationality comes to an impasse, *yet decisions must be made*. That said, not deciding is also a decision of sorts. Then, the matter is left just to "decide itself."

Years of experience

This critique of gut instinct should not, however, be mistakenly applied to decisions based on many years' experience in a particular area. Experienced managers are able to grasp and interpret complex situations more quickly than inexperienced ones. They tend to have considerable reserves of experiential knowledge to build on.

Yet highly experienced people in particular do not rely on their feelings. For they have also made the experience that they often enough misjudged a situation, or would have done if they had followed their gut. Among the thousands of high and highest-level executives with whom I have worked on complex decisions, only few made the most important decisions guided by gut feeling. The vast majority were far too responsible and aware of the risks.

Quick and thus largely spontaneous decisions are often enough explained by *intuition*, and indeed it is tempting even for the best managers to take pride in their intuition. Yet truly good managers feel ambivalent about this. No doubt there is such a thing as intuition and the strong feeling of subjective certainty that accompanies it. But the problem is not the existence or otherwise of intuition. The problem – as I have already said – is knowing in advance which of our intuitions are accurate and which will turn out to be *wrong*. Subjective certainty may be a strong emotion, but it is also a dangerous adviser. For it can just as easily be wrong as right. Of course it is possible that decisions are made too slowly, to the organization's detriment. Yet it is just as likely for a rash gut decision to wreak disaster. Balancing speed and thoroughness is one of those management problems that cannot be solved with recourse to a simple formula. What it takes are *judgment* (which can be sharpened), *experience* (which takes time to acquire), and a great deal of *expertise* (for which witticisms are no substitute).

The "inner voice" as advisor

I will after all make one recommendation in favor of something that might be called intuition, and which is useful for taking the *last* – not the first – step in a decision-making process. My advice to managers is to give themselves, when all analyses and deliberations have come to an end, an opportunity to heed the advice of a very special and remarkably cheap consultant: *their inner voice*.

In order to do so, one must give the inner voice a chance to speak up. *How* is up to the individual. Some people may want "to sleep on it." When your inner voice, particularly after the most scrupulous process of reaching a decision, clearly says, "something's not right," I would advise taking every opportunity to start from scratch. One could call this inner voice *intuition*. But I use the term with extreme caution in my own teaching. My reasons, in brief, are *first* that research has shown intuition to be wrong as often as right. Behavioral economics, as practiced by Ernst Fehr at the University of Zurich, and genetics promise some illuminating findings in this regard.

Second, because I do not believe intuition to be a luxury bestowed only on a privileged group of individuals. We all have something we call intuition: feelings, moods, hunches, inspirations. That's not the problem. The problem is to know *in advance* whose intuition will prove right in what situation.

Third, and this is the key difference: I accord intuition a different place in the decision-making process, not as a substitute for thought, but as its *touchstone*. Intuition should not be consulted at the beginning of a process, but at its *end*. It is not an easy way to get out of doing one's homework, but a controlling instance for when all the homework has been done and nothing more is to be gleaned from studying one's books. At this point, intuition is likely to be more helpful and reliable than it would be to follow one's first, spontaneous impulse.

ENTHUSIASM

Managers must be able to inspire enthusiasm in people – this is a commonplace opinion that often comes up in discussion, an axiom in any number of management books, and a criterion in many job searches and assessments. A positive relationship between enthusiasm and performance is assumed. The more enthusiastic people are about what they have to do, this assumption goes, the better they will perform. That sounds plausible enough, but where is the proof?

There is none. Any study would founder on the impossibility of measuring or operationalizing enthusiasm, nor can enthusiasm be produced for the purposes of an experiment. However convincing the supposed relationship between enthusiasm and performance may sound, it is pure superstition. In its place, I offer three propositions:

1. The more enthusiastic someone is, the less he or she is likely to know about the matter, and thus the more questionable are his or her abilities and performance.
2. Real performance, especially of the highest order, does not require enthusiasm; if anything, enthusiasm tends to get in the way. What is needed are competence, experience, and a lot of training.
3. Enthusiasm is not the cause, but often the consequence of great achievements.

Some people may find these propositions rather far-fetched, but they find ample confirmation. Most of us know people who are enthusiastic tennis players or skiers – without being very good at the sport. Others excel at them without mustering much enthusiasm. They take pleasure in the sport as long as it remains a hobby. Anyone engaged in sport professionally, as an athlete or as a coach, will be guided far more strongly by a sense of obligation and professionalism, maybe also ambition, or simply working out a contract. Of course victories spark enthusiasm and celebration. But what about defeats? They, too, are necessary in cultivating professionalism and preparing for victory.

Even the most interesting job cannot be done with consistent enthusiasm for a lifetime. Indeed, permanent enthusiasm is impossible to attain, for it wears off quickly. Let us consider the matter from another angle. Is enthusiasm necessary in order to do a job competently? Artisans, craftspeople, teachers, waiters, nurses, doctors, and managers in business all do not depend on enthusiasm to perform their tasks, nor is it helpful. What they need are professional skills, the mastery of their "craft."

Sport is a good sphere in which to study superlative achievement, especially professional sport, which comes with particular challenges. An experienced athlete enters a difficult contest with anything but enthusiasm, for what use would it be?

What helps athletes is the knowledge of having trained well, mastering their discipline, and being on good form. As a mountaineer, I have often found this to be true, and all accounts of difficult or extreme hikes bear out my experience. Only easier climbs allow something like enthusiasm to emerge. Even if preparing for an expedition or its early its early stages are done enthusiastically, this enthusiasm is not durable enough to take anyone to the summit. And it can occur only when one doesn't have a long and arduous descent ahead, which is often the most difficult part and again required performance and skill. No, enthusiasm is not a category that precedes achievement and for achievement. Enthusiasm is what comes after.

VALUE

Rarely before has a term seen such heavy use, and never, outside the confines of Marxist theory, have questions of value been accorded such centrality to the understanding of economic activity. The values I am speaking here are of an economic nature, not moral, ethical, or cultural. Such has been the intensity of its use and of the discussions the word has provoked that it has become easy to overlook the fact that there is no such thing as economic values. There are only prices.

The economic value of something, whatever it may be, is whatever the next buyer is prepared to pay for it. What the last buyer paid is of no consequence. Whatever one has paid oneself may influence one's own financial situation and thus one's thought, hopes, and bargaining tactics for the next transaction. Except as an idea, however, it is irrelevant. What is real are the next transaction and the price paid therein. Valuations, however they are arrived at, may suggest bargaining goals and influence hopes, desires, and placing orders on the stock market. And it is of course entirely possible that a previously calculated value actually turns out to be the price, at least for a while. This can give rise to the illusion that such valuations actually influence the asking price.

Yet every day, stock markets show that prices need bear no relation to actual valuations – and more often than not, they don't. To argue value, and thus whether a share or anything else happens to be over- or undervalued, is futile. There is no value beyond the price that the next buyer will pay. Based on this logic, it is similarly misguided to speak of "value chains" within a business, a term popularized by the American strategist and economist Michael E. Porter.[8] There are no values within a company, only costs. Only outside the company can costs be transformed into something of value – by a customer paying a price for goods or services.

To think in terms of value holds another danger, perhaps greater still. It exerts a dangerous pull on marketing, leading to the illusion that one's own efforts determine the product's value and thus its price. This would be to legitimize "cost-driven pricing." But the reality in the marketplace is the opposite, "price-driven costing."

To build a calculation by taking one's own costs as a starting point, adding a margin for risk and profit, and thus arriving at a price is almost invariably bound to fail in the marketplace. Only the actual market price can provide orientation. This price alone, once an appropriate profit margin has been subtracted, is the basis of all further calculations, from development to sales. This is the only way not to ignore the reality of the markets. The only reality in business is price.

DISRUPTION

The word "disruption" came into fashion with remarkable force and speed. Perhaps the media pounced on it so quickly because there was insufficient awareness of other terms that had long been used to describe the same phenomenon – only better. For the challenge denoted by disruption is far from new, but a historically recurring process of transformation on which there is a sizable body of research. It is a particular type of far-reaching change that can be observed to have followed the same pattern across the centuries.[9]

"Creative Destruction"

Not disruption, but "creative destruction" is the famous term coined by the Austrian economist Joseph Schumpeter to describe this special kind of change in which something existing is destroyed *by something creative and new*.

Taken by itself, change is nothing unusual. Innovation, improvement, and adaptation can be found everywhere. The technical term for what society and the economy are currently undergoing is "substitution." Its fundamental rule is: Whatever exists will be *replaced*. In 1997, when I was working on my book on corporate governance, which contained a sharp critique of the American shareholder-centric approach, I also wrote a chapter entitle "The Great Transformation." In it, I analyzed the socio-political and economic change that was already underway. Among my most important sources were Karl Polanyi and Peter F. Drucker, each of whom had already described such processes in his respective way.

"Transformation" is the title Drucker gave the introduction to his book *Post-Capitalist Society*, published in 1993, in which he analyzes the broad lines of development from capitalism to the knowledge economy, and from the nation-state to the transnational super-state. My own choice of terminology integrates some of the previous meanings to describe the universal and fundamental transformation taking place in the twenty-first century. This progress is marked by factors including exponentially growing complexity, the emergence of globally interconnected systems, and by the dynamic of self-accelerating change. What I described in my earlier book has largely become reality by now. But most likely we are only at the end of the first third of this fundamental transformation, which is far more than a paradigm shift. We are looking at a *categorical* change.

From the old world to a New World

What on the surface may look like a financial, economic, or debt crisis might be better understood in a larger dimension – not as the disruption of an old world, but as a *transformation* towards a New World, in which nearly everything will be unlike before. Economy and society are undergoing one of the greatest transformations history has ever seen. We are witnesses to the emergence of a fundamentally new order and a new way of functioning in society – a social ᴿEvolution of a new kind.

Such transformations have nothing to do with "social Darwinism," a concept widely and rightly decried. What this transformation accomplishes is to unlock higher levels of ability and capacity, and to a revolutionary degree. The steam engine – the symbol of the industrial revolution – did not, after all, destroy the draft animals of the time, but simply rendered them insignificant. It did not make horses and cows extinct, but stripped them of one of their purposes. They were no longer needed for traction and transport.

Transformation, not disruption

In times of transition, one of the most important things is to understand what is going on. Disruption only describes an unruly collapse or an arbitrary rupture. Transformation, by contrast, means something altogether different – Schumpeter's "creative destruction" or substitution. If one is familiar with these concepts, it is possible, amid the flood of facts and data, of information and events, to identify two fundamental patterns of change: The paradigm of the Great Transformation is two S-shaped curves overlying each other. They are S-shaped because they depict processes of growth and there are no such things as linear growth processes. What I have so far called the "old world" represents the *foundations of our world of tomorrow*. Between the curves lies the zone of increasing turbulence, in which the new supersedes the old. This is the *critical decision zone*; this is where transitions occur; this is where the old world comes apart and the New World begins to take shape.

Many things are no longer possible in the old world because it is coming to an end. A lot is *not yet* possible in the New World, because it is not yet fully formed or matured. For this very reason, it is all the more important, indeed a central task, for the leadership of every organization to find ways to make it work *nonetheless*.

INNOVATION

In the foreseeable future, innovations will be more important than ever. The future of nearly all organizations depends on them. But I cannot repeat myself too often: Most attempts at innovation fail. The proportion is eight out of ten, and the cost is horrendous. The main reason is that most businesses are seduced by the romance of innovation, but lack the corresponding professionalism in seeing them through. Each innovation is an expedition into uncharted territory, the first ascent of an imposing mountain. Yet all too often, they are embarked on as a walk in the park.

Market-based definition

Many managers are not even aware that they are in thrall to widespread errors and misapprehensions. The first such misapprehension is the notion that innovations are hatched in laboratories or R&D departments. What emerge from there are not innovations but ideas, or maybe prototypes and experimental results. Innovations, on the other hand, must be uncompromisingly defined with a view to the market. Only once marketing shows signs of success is it appropriate to speak of an innovation. This approach alone allows the right strategies to be chosen and investments of time and money to be estimated reasonably. The key question is not, "what have we developed, invented, or discovered?" but "what do we have to do to launch this development, invention, or discovery in the market successfully?"

No lack of ideas

The second mistake is the idea that creativity is important. As a result, creativity is a demanded of executives, businesses send their staff to creativity workshops, and "creative approaches" are applied throughout. Clearly, a fear has taken hold of being found to lack ideas. But not a lack of ideas is the problem, but a lack of *implemented* ideas. Even the most "uncreative" businesses have far more ideas than they ever put into practice.

To generate ideas is one thing, to implement them another. But only the latter can be called innovation. While the idea is not important, it is comparatively so, and certainly the cheapest and easiest part to come up with. The idea must be followed up by building a working prototype or carrying out clinical trials. All this takes far more time and effort. If the tests were successful, the development must be brought to the production stage, requiring further effort and expense. And finally, marketing must be begun. One can assume each subsequent step to require ten times the resources of the previous step.

The third fallacy is to believe that only small companies or "start-ups" can be creative. It is fashionable to decry the sluggishness of large corporations and to sing the praises of small entities. And indeed, small businesses can do much that large ones cannot. To innovate, however, is not one of these abilities. Smaller entities often are more creative, they are more receptive to new ideas and can reach the prototype stage sooner. But doing so often takes them to the limit of their energies. The stories of successful start-ups tend to obscure the much larger number of failures: Nine out ten vanish without much fanfare. Studies reveal the leading cause to be quite simple: "no market need."

Small companies usually have two problems: They have little money and are often poorly led. This makes many small, supposedly innovative companies interesting targets for takeovers by larger corporations. Small businesses are strong starters, but weak finishers. Yet effective innovation is not a sprint but a long-distance run, which requires endurance to make it through the second half of the race.

A fourth superstition is that innovation is always or primarily associated with high technology. The fascination exerted by technology has resulted in a fixation and thus in a collective blindness in other areas. No doubt the high-tech sector is growing, and with it the number of companies operating its various divisions. Yet this fixation risks overlooking the far more numerous possibilities opening up in non-technological areas, which frequently offer lucrative business opportunities at lower risk and with smaller investment.

The myth of the creative innovator

The fifth and most dangerous misconception is that to innovate is the preserve of a special type of person, the bold, creative, entrepreneurial, risk-happy pioneer. Such people exist, but they are rare. A closer look at supposed pioneers almost always reveals them to have been raised to that status retrospectively, styled heroes by adoring biographers or journalists.

Most genuine pioneers were in fact quite ordinary people. If anything, before they became successful, their contemporaries and associates tended to view them as eccentrics, deluded, or worse. There was nothing of the shining innovator about them. But they did usually have one asset: a systematic way of working. They knew their craft, their "stuff." Biographies hardly ever mention this, though it is the best lesson to be drawn from them.

GLOBALIZATION

The word "globalization" is used so often that one might think it was clear and unambiguous. Alas, that is not the case. Globalization has many meanings and can thus be used and abused almost at will.

Each business would thus be well advised to consider carefully what this word is supposed to mean and how one intends to use it. Even the more circumscribed term "internationalization" is far from clear. In how many countries does a country have to be present and do what percentage of its business there for it to be called "international"? There are no objective criteria. "International" need not refer to more than a mailbox in the Bahamas. "Multinational," too, lacks any specific meaning beyond having become a pejorative term for large corporations. Since the mid-1990s, Peter F. Drucker has been using the term "transnational" to describe those aspects independent of the nation state and national understanding. For the time being, Drucker considers only two things to be transnational: money and information.

The world is not a village

Globalization does not mean that the world is turning into a "village," for which conditions are entirely lacking. How is one to envisage a village with a population of more than seven billion? Even scare quotes will do nothing to make a "global village" of so vast a number of people. This should be as obvious to a child of the great cities as it is to someone who grew up in a small village. Globalization does not mean that the world's cultures should end up resembling each other, let alone "Western" ways of life and thought, which are themselves far from homogeneous. It even seems more probable that stronger emphasis will be placed on differences. Nor does globalization mean that every company or its products must be present in every country of this world. Even among the largest corporations, such names are few: Coca-Cola, for sure, but even Apple is less straightforward a case. Most companies have good reason to continue being selective about where to do business. So, for the time being, globalization means three things:

First, that no location can be dismissed out of hand as a potential site of economic activity. This means that every stage of economic activity – from development via procurement to sales – can, as a matter of principle, take place anywhere in the world. *Second*, that national borders no longer provide effective protection against completion, although a reawakening of protectionism cannot be excluded – on the contrary. *Third*, that a global view, global awareness, is necessary to avoid being surprised. Yet this does not mean that one should have to act globally. To my mind, the third aspect is the most important for businesses. Even in the remote future, not every company will have to operate globally. But more and more of them, including smaller businesses, will have to be globally informed. Only this can protect them from being wrong-footed by competitors or surprised by developments they might have anticipated, especially with regard to new developments in production and procurement. To cultivate this global view is quite difficult and requires some effort.

Entrepreneurs forced to consider the possibilities of the first point might benefit from consulting the history books when they are told of the novelty and uniqueness of today's globalization process. Nobody needed to tell the merchants of northern Italy in the fifteenth and sixteenth centuries that there was a world out there. In the Renaissance, Venetians and Florentines conducted business on a global scale. The German Fugger dynasty followed their example and set up a global network that lasted some 200 years. Their "factors," as their local representatives were called, were present in all the known world's major countries and cities, did business throughout Europe, and controlled half of South America – all without the benefit of the internet, smartphones, and airplanes – and were able to weather the bankruptcies of the Habsburg monarchs. The religious order of Jesuits, too, was active as a global trading and knowledge network extending to Japan and China, India and Latin America. Their success was such that they attracted much suspicion and hostility, being proscribed in several countries.

Globalization is older than the internet. It has seen golden ages and experienced setbacks. The main lesson its history has to teach the leaders of today's organizations may well be this: practice sound judgment.

COMPLEXITY

Until recently the preserve of specialists in computer science and cybernetics, "complexity" is now the height of fashion. Yet the word's frequent use has done nothing to add to its understanding. This is destined to change, for "complexity" is *the* key word to understanding the digital world.

Few people and organizations today are already prepared to deal adequately with complexity. Evidence can be found in the fact that most people want to *reduce* complexity. They see complexity as something chiefly negative. In their search for simple solutions, they apply the strategy of complexity reduction. Yet such thinking is almost invariably the result of confusing complexity with complication. As a result, truly viable solutions are ignored and crises inadvertently exacerbated. For mounting complexity – in fact, its explosive growth – is the single greatest challenge facing global societies and their organizations.

Complexity is not complication

Complexity is the most fundamental property of reality – its diversity. Complexity is the natural and inevitable consequence of interconnectedness. And interconnectedness, in turn, produces new and unforeseeable phenomena. The consequences of complexity are impenetrability, incalculability, non-analyzability, unpredictability, and uncontrollable continuous change. But all the higher faculties that biological and social systems can display, like adaptability, learning skills, flexibility, responsiveness, evolvability, creativity, communicativeness, consciousness, and identity result from complexity. These results may make management difficult, yet when handled correctly, they open up hitherto unimaginable possibilities for business as well as society at large.

Utilizing complexity as a new raw material

The correct maxim goes: *Reduce complication and increase complexity*. As the German biologist Carsten Bresch put it so well: "All higher abilities result from greater complexity!" Complexity is a new raw material, maybe even the most valuable. For complexity is the stuff from which are made intelligence, creativity, innovation, and evolution, self-regulation and self-organization, as biological and, increasingly, electronic systems show. So instead of casting about for simple solutions by reducing complexity, we would do better to find intelligent solutions by making use of existing complexity. Fortunately, it will turn out that the intelligent solution also happens often to be the simplest, whereas simple solutions need not be intelligent.

GOVERNANCE

The term "governance" and its roots cover much of what constitutes right and good management. Both the Latin *gubernare* and the Greek κυβερνάω mean "to steer," in a nautical context, to be in command of a vessel, to be at its helm. And that is what management should be in the best systems-cybernetic sense: to steer, guide, control, handle, and balance. All the more so since the reality facing navigators and helmsmen is highly complex: unpredictable, incalculable, and subject to constant change. Such circumstances call for leadership that is evolutionary, not rigid; complex, not facile; interconnected, not separated; simultaneous, not sequential.

In my book on corporate policy and governance (2007), I explain why governance is the term of choice for the systems-cybernetic management of businesses and other organizations. When I wrote my first book on corporate governance in 1997, the time was not yet right, for the concept of governance was tied to that of shareholder value. Yet to allow a company's strategic orientation to follow shareholder value alone has little to do with governance in the cybernetic sense.

The original definition by the Cadbury Committee for Corporate Governance (1992) did not mention cybernetics, but tallies with my opening thoughts: *Corporate Governance is the system by which companies are run.* Complexity was not yet an issue, and the first signs of the imminent transformation had barely been recognized. The first mass-market web browser was launched in 1994, the iPhone another 13 years later. Digitalization as we know it was only just beginning; the global market leader in photography was still Kodak, with annual sales of $ 20 billion. Under the influence of the growth of the stock market and the New Economy, the prevailing definition of corporate governance became a caricature of good practice. Center stage was now taken not by long-term goals, but by shareholder value, which was expressed in the latest share price. The maximization of corporate value as seen through the lens of the stock market was the sole valid criterion. The customer was pushed aside by the shareholder. Years of unimaginable financial excess, manipulated accounts, and grotesque bonuses ensued.

Under the impression not least of the collapse of Lehman Brothers and its implications for the global finance system, a movement took hold for reform of governance codes, in order to reduce the likelihood of the events of the 1990s and 2000s repeating. This is a good start, though further repairs are necessary. Today's corporate governance codes regulate both too little and too much. Too many of their recommendations are wrong, too few are right. Not enough attention is paid to the perspective of corporate management itself, the actual problems of steering and guidance. For the practical application of corporate governance codes and their compliance rules leads to massive restrictions on the highest executive bodies, which takes them further and further from their actual tasks. Executive bodies can devote less care to the company's wellbeing and more to compliance with legal rules, caution with regard to the business media, attention to short-term investor interests, and protecting themselves from personal liability claims. The priority of formal governance rules has spelled a marked decline in entrepreneurial courage, risk-taking, and far-sightedness.

Tentative attempts at reform are no less misguided in reviving so-called stakeholder approaches. Yet it was the *failure* of these very approaches that ushered in the dominance of the equally unsuited shareholder principle. Concepts like corporate social responsibility and corporate citizenship, to which reforms try to do justice, are completely justified, because the shareholder approach not only ignored, but systematically infringed on them. The suggested measures, however, are not yet well enough thought out. A different path needs to be taken. There can be no doubt as to the purpose that should guide a business and to which it should adhere if is to remain strategically and operationally successful: "The purpose of a business is to create a customer." Peter F. Drucker formulated this thought, so clear and true, in his book *The Practice of Management* – as early as 1954.

From management to self-management, from organization to self-organization

Corporate governance is an *all-encompassing systems policy*, which triggers the evolutionary leap from regulation to self-regulation by making use of the forces lying dormant within the system. To guide, steer, and regulate are just other words for managing, and at heart they all mean the same thing: to create order where otherwise there would be none, and to give direction where it is lacking. Regulation is done by means of rules. To regulate in accordance with the system always follows the same logic, as it is presented here.

In the cybernetic sense, then, governance means: *Manage a system in such a way that it can manage, regulate, and organize itself, that it is enabled to release its power and potential, and that it is able to adapt to new and unknown situations.* Entrepreneurs and experienced managers have always known that a business is more than an economic machine for growth, and they acted accordingly, or their businesses would not have worked at all. Now, there is a good chance of a new corporate governance emerging, which will place the customer and the business itself back at the center of management. After some three decades of confusion, the concept of corporate government is restored to its rightful place and its true meaning.

GROWTH

Although it is unquestionably an important consideration in business, as a strategic target growth is wrong and
dangerous. It can all too easily lead a business to failure –
even while the analysts applaud.

Growth must not be the input for a strategy, but its
output. And growth must not be set as a target at the out-
set, but instead is the result of thinking through business
and its inner laws and patterns. Growth begins with customer utility. As long as that fact is not firmly secured in
the minds of executive and supervisory bodies, the same
mistake will keep being made. An advanced level of strategic planning is reached only when a distinction is made
between healthy and sick growth: a twelve-year-old who
grows an inch or two each year is healthy; a fifty-year-old
doing the same would clearly be abnormal.

Size as such must never be a strategic target. A business need not be large, but it must be strong. There is
no imaginable constellation in which a company's size is
strategically important. To look at size alone is to fall
prey to an optical illusion and no longer be able to tell
flab from muscle. The confusion arises because the right
strategies may almost always lead to growth and thus
size, but the reverse does not follow. Size may also the result of the wrong strategies.

Size is measured in terms of sales and turnover, and,
though nowadays rather less often, workforce. Turnover
can be increased with relative ease if one allows this to
happen the wrong way, for instance by geographic ex-

pansion, launching new products, or by the wrong mergers and acquisitions. Without exception, the results are: complexity mounts, manageability erodes, and profitability diminishes. Absolute numbers go up, and by sheer dint of their visibility are mistaken for signs of success. Matters look different on the balance sheet; ratios decline – but go unnoticed.

There are only two measures by which reliably to distinguish healthy growth from sick. The first is market position: Size and growth are healthy only if they are the result of an increased market position in the relevant sectors. Conversely, growth and size taken alone do not automatically bring about a stronger market position. A large company can still have a small and weak position in all or many markets. The second indicator, more important still, is productivity. Only the best-run businesses possess instruments sophisticated enough to measure productivity. Productivity continues to be neglected, poorly defined, and wrongly measured. Yet, as "total factor productivity," it is the only reliable indicator by which to assess growth. Only when growing turnover is reflected in growing overall productivity are we looking at healthy growth, building muscle and strength. If, on the other hand, the overall productivity of a growing business stagnates, then all it is putting on is fat. A bit of flab needn't do any harm – up to a point. When overall productivity declines in spite of growth, a business might be said to have cancer. Tumors can grow fast, killing the patient. Only at the early stages can this development be corrected – sometimes.

CONTROL

When something is under control, does this suggest the presence of a controller? And does something traveling in the right direction point to there being someone at the steering wheel? Or are these mere optical illusions? The distinction is as simple as it is important: Simple systems may be controlled in a number of ways, but complex systems require control as defined by cybernetics.

Is control really necessary?

For quite some time now, "control" has labored under almost exclusively negative connotations. To be a "control freak" is to suffer from a morbid lack of trust, and individuals perceived to be "controlling" cause much resentment. Yet contrary to widespread belief, managers do not relish exercising control. It is, in fact, one of their least popular tasks. Some managers simply don't enjoy it, others aren't sure how best to go about it, and another group is afraid of being thought autocratic. People who advise against control can thus expect a warm welcome, regardless of the cogency of their arguments. They are heard and indeed praised in the media as pioneers of a new style of hands-off management.

Yet a correct understanding of control is indispensable. It is a gross misapprehension to imagine a controller as an organ of surveillance or inspection. Such an emphasis makes control in management a dangerous word and ends up being counterproductive.

In order to safeguard the quality and effectiveness of leadership, it would be irresponsible to advise against control. Whether or not to exercise control is simply not a matter for discussion. The important question is *how* best to do it.

Among the arguments often leveled against control are that people dislike being controlled, that it harms motivation, and that it curtails precious freedoms. And it is true that many people don't much care for being controlled – myself included. But does it follow that control is not necessary in many situations? After all, people dislike all manner of things that may nonetheless be important, or indeed for that very reason. Many of the scandals in the world of business and finance might have been prevented had thorough control been exercised, and the same is true for road, rail, and air accidents, or disasters in tunnels and power stations. Almost invariably, incomplete or lackadaisical control carries at least part of the blame. And many students might not have failed their exams if their knowledge had been controlled earlier …

"Control can harm motivation" – true enough, but by no means inevitable. Demotivating control happens more often than it should. And there are cases, albeit fairly rare, of control being abused for power play or even harassment. But this is not sufficient reason to forego control. They are management errors that simply must be rooted out, which it why mangers should be examined as to whether they control and how.

"Control curtails freedoms" – this argument just misses the point. Control does not mean having "no freedom," no room or leeway to do as one sees fit. Whether such freedoms are necessary, where they are to be created, to whom they should apply, where not to grant them – these are all questions that have almost nothing to do with control. They are matters of an organization's type and structure, and all too often with its ideology, too.

Self-control, self-regulation

Given that control is necessary, let us consider its various forms. The best is effective self-control, which means enabling as many people in an organization as possible to control themselves as far as possible. Control in its cybernetic sense means the ability of complex systems to regulate, organize, heal, and reproduce *themselves* according to circumstances, i.e. internal and external effects. In nature, the self-regulation of organisms and ecosystems is the norm. Typical examples include the cardio-pulmonary-system as it adapts to varying physical stress, the digestive process, and the adaptive self-regulation of the sensory organs.

Control denotes existing or created and evolving mechanisms (i.e. rules) that allow for the purposeful utilization of complexity, the functioning of systems, and their ability to withstand error. Hence, in its cybernetic sense, control means more than the superficial meaning involved in having a situation "under control" or exercising "control over" something. The system is not just *under* control, but it steers and regulates itself in such a manner that it is able to fulfill its purpose, undo or compensate for faults, and evolve. To put in biological terms, it can survive and remain viable, the way that wounds below a certain severity heal themselves, cells grow back, a population sustains itself by reproduction, and the mechanisms of alarm, flight and defense respond, as it were, autonomously to threats.

Cybernetic controls for organizations include what I refer to as "master controls," which are the fundamental rules that apply throughout a system, all the way to its most peripheral elements. And they do so regardless of their source, be they laws of nature – structural circumstances, or man-made – regulative decisions or principles.

For the most important master controls for effective leadership are decisions and principles that implant a system's autonomous capacities, which are self-regulation, self-organization, self-steering, and self-guiding. Such decisions include well thought-out mission statements, strategies, and communication and feedback systems.

Control by communication

To rid oneself of control's negative associations with "inspection"–a misunderstanding that stands in the way of effective management – and instead to understand control in the cybernetic sense discussed above, is also to bid farewell to a philosophy that implicitly assumes the presence of a "helmsman" or even "controller." For such an idea of deliberate, targeted, or planned external steering interventions is not just an obstacle, but counterproductive and wrong.

142

Properly understood steering or control is the property of systems that have reached a certain level of complexity, which they would be unable to maintain without the autonomous abilities discussed above and which, in turn, they need to sustain these abilities.

Just as the human body would be unable to function without its nervous system, an organization cannot work without processes that steer and regulate it. Our nervous system is the equivalent of the management processes. That is where the cybernetics of functioning takes place, which is to say, the steering and regulation of transactions on the business or operational level. That, too, is where nerves transmit communication, which steers processes. Thus, *control by communication* is the true definition of cybernetics. The mere question how this might be accomplished is of considerable value. To think it through can lead to what is often a radically altered and improved understanding of an organization.

But even this would not do away with the necessity for control. After all, whether self-control works should be controlled from time to time. Speed controls in traffic provide a good illustration: All cars are equipped to allow drivers to control and check their speed. Yet as we know, they are not always used as intended.

Founded on trust

Control in management must be founded on trust, trust first and foremost in two things: human capacity and human willingness. If one cannot even trust in these two conditions being met, then the problem is not one of control, but perhaps one of staffing or personnel.

Yet this trust, too, must not be blind, but justified. One should trust as far as possible, maybe even further than one's comfort zone extends, but one must also ensure that violations of trust are discovered, that people know they will be discovered, and that such breaches will entail severe and non-negotiable consequences.

The question thus cannot be, *what are all the things we can possibly control?*, but instead: *What must we – absolutely and indispensably – control in order to have sufficiently founded trust that nothing crucial can get out of hand, because its own mechanisms of self-correction are built into the system?*

TRUST

The word "trust" as such is not dangerous, but there are three dangers associated with it. The first is to overlook the significance of trust in favor of a fixation on motivation. The second is to make trust an emotional or even a psychological issue. And the third is to confuse trust with credulity, with blind confidence.

Some managers do everything wrong – by the yardstick of conventional wisdom – and yet can enjoy an excellent situation in their organizations and domains of responsibility, a good working climate, and able and efficient workers. And then there are others who follow the book and the business coaches' teachings, heed the seminars on leadership and motivation, and nonetheless arrive at the opposite result: A tense mood in their departments, frustrated staff, and a corporate culture that seems to discourage performance. How to explain such a discrepancy?

Examination of individual cases almost invariably reveals the critical aspects not to be motivation and leadership style, but the question whether or not staff trust their boss. If managers succeed in winning the trust of their associates, their colleagues, staff, and superiors, other factors are left to play comparatively insignificant parts. Such managers have succeeded in creating what I call a robust leadership situation: robust in the face of the many errors of leadership, conduct, and motivation that happen from day to day.

This is not to excuse or justify those errors, but happen

they do – even to the best managers, entirely by accident and often unnoticed. Just as they do to most other people. The question thus ceases to be whether or not mistakes are made, but what impact they make. Organizations must be quite "thick-skinned" if they are to work. Businesses, and well-managed ones in particular, are not touchy-feely places. There is no time to weigh each word several times over, and if everything that is said or left unsaid were constantly questioned, normal functioning would soon come to a halt.

An organization depends on a minimum of mutual trust for anything to work. The logic of the matter is as simple as it is compelling: If and as long as there is trust, one need not be unduly worried about motivation, working climate, and corporate culture. This is not to say that these points are unimportant. But what is more important is to be aware that any attempts to address them will be futile if trust is found to be lacking. Worse still, they can produce the opposite of the result intended. Measures to increase motivation and improve corporate culture then end up being received as particularly subtle forms of manipulation and ultimately as cynical. Trust is not the only, but certainly the most important foundation for any form of leadership that is reasonable, in line with human needs, and above all functioning.

The second danger: Contrary to common opinion, trust and its opposite, distrust, are not emotional phenomena, though both are associated with certain feelings. It is also unnecessary to speak of a "culture of trust" or a "culture of distrust," which has become something of a kneejerk response.

Trust of the kind important in relation to leadership emerges not from certain states of feeling, though it might contribute to them, but from *the logic of a situation*. It results from *consistent* behavior, reliability, and integrity of character. That seems like a big word, but it means something quite simple, well within every manager's reach: *To mean what you say and act accordingly, and to keep your promises.*

Make no mistake: First, to mean what you say does not entail *saying everything you mean*. In the real world of our organizations, that would be foolish. As a leader, it important to consider what one says, in front of whom, and when. But when you decide to say something, you must be sincere. And, second, this does not mean that you can never change your mind. You can, and you will likely have to do so more often than before, because the organization's situation will change more rapidly than ever. But it is important to say that you have changed your mind and, if good leadership is your goal, to explain the reasons for changing your mind.

It does not follow from the above that trust replaces or is the same as motivation. Their relation is different: Of course it is all the better if trust is supplemented by motivation. As a rule, to motivate is not much of a problem under such conditions. The significance of the above observation is revealed by the negative case, the absence of trust, when efforts to motivate are futile. Any attempts will be in vain in the absence of a modicum of trust and, as I have already said, are likely to have undesirable results.

Trust does not replace motivation. Trust works as a catalyst. Motivation can only be effective where trust is already in place. For this reason, so many well-meaning and indeed scientifically competent motivational programs, much to their initiators' surprise, are doomed to ineffectiveness or turn out to be counterproductive.

RESPONSIBILITY

As long as the meaning and function of management are unclear or keep changing according to the vagaries of fashion, no suitable answers will be found to the fundamental question of responsibility in management. But once it has become clear what right and good management is, the answers will be self-evident. This puts clear guidelines at our disposal. To apply them, however, is an *entirely personal decision*.

What one decides to do

Responsibility requires something I call "everyday ethics." This means answering for one's actions – and for one's omissions. This is based on personal decision everyone must one day make not to run away from responsibility.

Managers are, first, responsible for themselves, their own performance, and their own success. Second, they are responsible for others, their staff, and their performance and success. Third, managers are responsible for their institution, its performance, and its success. They are responsible for ensuring that everyone can work to the best of their abilities by utilizing their strengths. The concrete meaning of these responsibilities becomes apparent when they are measured against the purpose of the institution, for that is their yardstick.

The manager's responsibility

Managers are responsible for exercising their function with the highest degree of professionalism possible. They cannot bear responsibility for what they can influence neither directly nor indirectly. Managers are not responsible for changing people, least of all for changing their personalities. To change oneself is a personal choice everybody is free to make. Right management presupposes neither supermen nor saints. To raise expectations in accordance with such ideas leads to the opposite of right management.

Furthermore, managers are responsible for acquiring the relevant expertise in their field of business and in management itself if they are not to find themselves hampered at every step. They can and ought to be expected to be capable of separating being from appearance, content from packaging, right from wrong, and the functional from the merely fashionable. A manager unable to make these distinctions is not (yet) sufficiently professional and can put his or her institution at risk. Managers in key positions let the following question guide their decisions, knowing full well that compromise will be required: *What, in this situation, is the right thing for the company?*

It is my belief that managers bear the additional responsibility of representing the function of management in public, and in such a way to allow people to understand it. This responsibility is not fulfilled by making after-dinner speeches or by showing off to TV audiences. One does so by one's own results and one's personal example. Only they have the power truly to convince. A special responsibility falls to the representatives of major corporations, who are widely visible in the media. Rightly or not, these major corporations determine the public image of business and management. They are perceived as representing business as a whole.

Managers are responsible for their actions not arousing hostility towards business and not provoking any measures that now or in future would place burdens or restrictions on the functioning of the economy. They are responsible for showing by their actions that healthy businesses require a healthy economy and a healthy society. In doing so, managers fulfill their responsibility by showing people that business is not, as some would have it, too important to be left to managers, but too important to be left to *bad* managers.

CUSTOMER

The danger in the word "customer" lies in disregarding it and thus losing sight of what is most important to any business, its *raison d'être*. Had someone told me, at the beginning of the 1990s, that this was going to be the exact case for the next twenty or so years, I would not have believed it. But that is what came to pass under the doctrine of shareholder value. And that is the principal cause of the accounting scams and bankruptcies, the financial troubles and bailouts, that were first hinted at in the stock market crash of March 2000. More was to come.

The doctrine of shareholder value, by placing the interests of investors front and center, legitimized what was in fact a turn away from customers and their needs. It also gave a particular personality type the chance to rise to the top, namely the kind of manager for whom only quantifiable measures – worse: quantifiable only in terms of money – carried any weight. In doing so, the doctrine of shareholder value inaugurated an era of stunted leadership and one-dimensional management.

What had once been justly lauded as advances in the study of management could now be ignored with the support of "science." That businesses can be understood only as complex, multi-dimensional systems – meaning, in turn, that management meant mastering the ability to weigh and balance out numerous, often contradictory factors – could be pushed aside. Leadership was suddenly made easy, because success was daily evident in stock market prices, which, to the minds of the historically illiterate, could only continue rising.

The key findings of the study of strategy, which holds that successful strategy means serving markets and customers better than competitors can, could equally be thrown to the wind. Strategy now consisted in cutting deals and living up to the expectations of the stock market, analysts, and the media.

Marxists and communists aside, nobody had previously denied the well-defined interest and the concomitant right of shareholders to see a return on their investment. What is no less clear is that this can be achieved only by way of the satisfied customer, and that it should be in the interest of shareholders to focus attention there.

Economic activity is complex in practice, but its logic is quite simple: A business with customers will always be able to obtain capital, be it from the stock market or elsewhere. But as the New Economy showed, no amount of capital will make for a viable business in the absence of customers. The ability of an idea to attract capital on the stock market is no indication of its use to customers. Yet customers, not shareholders, are the people who pick up the tab. In a manner of speaking, shareholders pay the check only if and when a business has failed in its foremost task: to look for, find, and satisfy customers. Customer orientation is about creating output, whereas shareholder orientation is about distributing gains. The former is the difficult part, the latter is easy.

RISK-TAKING

The call for risk-taking, dynamic entrepreneurs and start-up-founders has hardly ever been heard as loudly has it has these past few years. To many minds, the visionary, creative pioneer, willing to take chances wherever they may offer themselves, is the driving force behind the new digital economy. Silicon Valley is the much heralded, shining example. The fact that for every successful company, dozens if not hundreds of ventures fail seems not to be present in many minds. Yet such are the laws of evolution.

Success is impossible to achieve without taking risks. This is true not only for business, but probably for all pioneering deeds humans have ever performed. But there are many kinds of risk. Only by distinguishing them clearly can one hope to make right decisions.

The different kinds of risk

First, there is the inevitable risk associated with any kind of economic activity. Life itself, as we know, is a risky business, and business itself is full of risks. They are far greater than most people can imagine, because modern society insures them against making the necessary, usually painful, experiences. Yet every New Year's Eve, regardless of how good the year was, all counters are set back to zero and the struggle begins anew.

People who have to balance the books, especially if

their own money is at stake, know that and are thus habitually wary of others exhorting them to take more risks. This is not to be lacking in courage. Even the ordinary risk involved in doing business is considerable, for it is *always* the risk of failure.

The second kind of risk is the additional risk that one can afford to take – or just about. One can afford it because one can expect to survive failure. Most entrepreneurs need little encouragement to take such risks. Someone who earns a hundred thousand a year and visits a casino with a thousand in his pocket is likely to lose his money, but can be expected to get over it. In fact, the stake is not one thousand, but fifteen hundred – tax having presumably been paid on his income – but that, too, is a probably a bearable loss.

The third kind of risk is the additional risk that one most certainly *cannot* afford, because it will be fatal if the bet falls through. On no account, under no conditions must such a risk be taken, however great the chance of success and the gains may seem, and however much bystanders may goad you.

This does not mean that such transactions should not, as a matter of principle, be contemplated at all. But rather than trying to work out probabilities, mental energy would be better spent thinking about how a risk of the third kind might be converted into one of the second – for instance, by working on the terms of the contract or taking partners on board.

For want of a choice?

Finally, a fourth kind of risk: the risk that one *cannot* afford *not* to take. It is the risk that *must* be taken because one has no choice in the matter. The term for this is not calculated risk or the usual entrepreneurial risk – it is fate, inevitability, or tragedy. Greek tragedy and Shakespeare's greatest plays dramatize this kind of risk, which makes them exciting, fascinating, and – tragic. The excitement should end, however, at the door of one's own company. Perhaps such risks follow from earlier errors and from ignoring the iron rules of management. One may once foolishly have said A, B, and C and now has no choice but to accept X, Y, and Z.

These four types of risk, at least, should be distinguished – including by those who would so loudly clamor for risk-happy entrepreneurs, often from what is itself a largely risk-free position. Nobody benefits from the collapse of a business. Without exception, it spells the destruction of productivity and wealth. Above all, for young people to be lured into taking the wrong kinds of risk destroys any commitment and motivation to do business responsibly.

FUN

Should work be fun? Does it have to be for us to be motivated? Nowadays, these questions are usually answered in the affirmative. As plausible as it may sound, it is a problematic attitude, because it tends to be taken not as a wish, but as a demand, even an entitlement. Belief in this entitlement has become widespread – with questionable consequences. For it has created expectations that virtually no organization can meet in the long run. Of course it is possible for work in businesses and other organizations to be fun, but in a different way and for different reasons.

Unrealistic expectations

The call for fun in the workplace should be filed under "plausible (superficially)." In reality, it makes it difficult, sometimes even impossible, to motivate the workforce in a solid, sustainable, and reasonable way. Moreover, it sets in motion a vicious circle: The expectations raised by executives and coaches are disappointed and staff end up frustrated. The response is to lie on even more motivational schemes, which may, however, be perceived as manipulation, a cynical ploy, because it changes nothing about working reality. Yet the demand for fun remains while frustration mounts, because people feel they are being taken for a ride. It is not easy to break this vicious circle, but it can be done with the courage to proclaim a new realism.

More differentiation

To begin, it might be worth calling to mind that the call for fun in the workplace was first heard only a few decades ago and represents a historic novelty. This does nothing to change the demand or the promise, but it does put them into perspective. Second, it would be useful to recall the distinction between joy and pleasure. They are not the same thing, and many languages these terms separate for good reason. Work can bring pleasure even if is not "fun" in the usual sense of the word.

Let us consider the opposite terms: Of course everything should be done to alleviate the pain, suffering, and distress associated with work wherever possible. The developed nations have made enormous progress in this area over the last century and a half. Taken as a whole, these measures form one of the revolutions whose history remains to be written. It is equally self-evident that progress has been made if more and more kinds of work can, at least sometimes, be pleasurable. Yet it should be understood that no job can be pleasurable *all the time*, and that, conversely, every job probably has aspects in which nobody would ever find pleasure.

Even occupations that many might imagine to be wonderfully exciting or fascinating jobs – maybe pilot, actor, or orchestral conductor – have tiresome sides to them. They, too, entail a considerable measure of routine, boredom, and struggle, which come at the expense of pleasure.

I once had the opportunity to discuss this matter with one of the most famous orchestral conductors, naively assuming that such a wonderful job, and music as such, must bring him daily pleasure. The long, silent look he gave me was almost unbearable. He then said quietly: "I've conducted tonight's Mozart symphony so often that I can no longer bear the sound of it. It gives me a rash just to say its name." After another long pause, he added: "But the orchestra won't notice a thing tonight – let alone the audience ...".

It should also be understood that even such jobs need to be done that not only have onerous sides to them, but which as a whole are unlikely ever to bring much joy or pleasure to anyone. We cannot yet foresee what advances in digitalization and robotics will change about this. But for time being, lavatories will have to be cleaned and refuse collected, along with all manner of menial tasks that will never be the slightest bit "fun." What are the people doing these jobs to make of the demand that work should be fun?

The same question applies to people whose work brings them into daily contact with the word's suffering and ills: people who work with refugees, but find there is only so much they can do; social workers who can at best treat the symptoms of drug abuse and homelessness; teachers in inner-city schools; doctors and nurses in intensive or palliative care wards, working with the odds stacked against them. They all work not for pleasure, but because the job needs to be done. Though it may sound hopelessly old-fashioned: They do the job because they see it as their duty and responsibility.

Work or results?

The demand for work to be pleasurable or even fun leads not only to intractable motivational problems. There is a second negative, indeed fatal, consequence. It distracts from the most important aspect of work, the very aspect that makes solutions possible: its *results*.

It diverts people's attention from the work as such rather than orienting them towards their work's *results*. As important as work may be, the results are more so – not input, but output.

If one is in the business of making demands, one would do better to demand that not work should bring pleasure, but its results. Results should make people proud, give them satisfaction and a sense of purpose. Even if work itself is most certainly not fun, then pleasure and at least a hint of satisfaction may be drawn from the outcomes. Rightful pride may be felt in the fruits of even the most menial tasks and contribute to the self-respect that is a legitimate human need.

As long as it's meaningful ...

Managers should enable people to do work important to the organization, make use of their strengths, and give them the opportunity to turn in their best performance. Usually, that's all it takes. We pay for performance and not for that performance's reasons or motivations, or for the feelings associated with it. We could not do so even if we wanted to, because we have no way of knowing them well enough.

The most important thing is to give people the chance to find meaning in their activities though their outcomes. Victor Frankl, the master theoretician of meaning in life, put it terms that I find entirely convincing: Meaning is decisive, not self-fulfillment. Even Abraham Maslow, the most famous of motivational psychologists, agreed and responded by removing self-fulfillment from the peak of his motivational pyramid. Alas, this fact is too little known, which is why the outdated version is still widely taught.

The efforts of good, *effective* managers are directed at giving people tasks whose meaning there are able to recognize – tasks that have meaning to them. Meaning is the decisive, the most durable and effective motivator. All others pale in significance beside it. If someone claims to find fun or pleasure in their work, they deserve congratulations. It is a privilege in every respect, and it is a rarity. If only enjoyable jobs continued to be doe, society would collapse within twelve hours. What counts is the ability to take pride in the results of one's work, in one's own achievements, and – above all – to find meaning in them.

CONCENTRATION

The principle of concentration is so important to management because no other profession is so intensely and systematically exposed to the dangers of powers becoming tied up and fragmented. These dangers apply to other spheres as well, but nowhere are they as institutionalized as in management and so "respectable," which is to say misunderstood as a sign of particular energy, dynamism, and ability. Yet in fact, nothing is as typical of effective mangers as their ability to concentrate on a just few things, but truly important ones.

The word "concentration" alone is not enough. That is why is deserves a place among this list of dangerous words. The crucial point to observe in the pursuit of efficacy and success is to restrict oneself to a small number of well-chosen priorities. The choice of priorities requires care, conscientiousness, a thorough assessment of the situation – and practical experience. Objections are sometimes voiced that the principle of concentration could not be applied to complex and interconnected situations. Yet the exact reverse is true.

Only because so much is complex, interconnected, and interactive is this principle important. It was not always thus – for a very simple reason: It was of no use in simple situations. Where there are no distractions, the principle automatically applies. No farmer plowing a field or worker in a steel mill was ever subject to the temptation of getting sidetracked that is so typical of modern-day knowledge workers, and managers in particular. The situation is clear: Of course it is possible to deal with many things at once. What is not possible, however, is to be successful in many different areas. It is thus necessary to distinguish between work and performance, being busy and being successful.

Wherever efficacy, success, and results are in evidence, it can be safely assumed – some lucky exceptions notwithstanding – that the principle of concentrating on just a few things has been observed. Nearly all people who have in some way attained recognition or even fame for their achievements did so by concentrating on one thing, one objective, one problem. This can reach the point of obsession, even becoming pathological – not a course I would advise. Yet it always holds true that the key to outcomes is the concentration on a single thing or a select few. This is true even of ordinary outcomes, how much more so – with no exception or compromise – for extraordinary achievements.

In the annals of reasonably well-documented history, only two individuals come to mind whose tried their hand at many different things – sometimes simultaneously – and did so successfully, at least in the estimation of posterity. Their names are Leonardo da Vinci and Johann Wolfgang von Goethe. Yet in both cases it might be argued that they, too, often got sidetracked and could have achieved more and greater things if they had restricted themselves a little. That they nevertheless achieved greatness is due to their exceptional gifts. But what manager can claim in good faith to come close to Leonardo or Goethe?

CORPORATE SUCCESS

Troubled times require standards that are clear, unambiguous, and impervious to fashion. What makes good business? When is a company healthy? How can success and failure be reliably assessed? The more significance is accorded to financial indicators, the more important is to see the bigger picture.

There are six key indicators for corporate success. Only taken together and over the course of a longer period do they allow conclusions to be drawn about the state of a company – but those conclusions will be precise and reliable. Collectively, I think of these indicators as the managers' "dashboard." They are also the key factors for any corporate strategy.

The first indicator is a company's *market position* in relation to the areas in which it does business. There is no single measure that would suffice for this purpose. Usually, much attention is paid to market share, but how to define it? Geographically or by customer demographics, by distribution channel or intended purpose, with regard to direct customers or the retail market? Is the market share of comparable products known, and what about quality and utility, brand familiarity and image?

Each company must consider what factors adequately describe its own particular market position and develop the appropriate measurements. Constantly to improve market position as a whole, and not just market share, but be at the center of every corporate strategy. One can barely go wrong with this.

The second indicator is *innovativeness*. Companies that have ceased to innovate are almost irreversibly doomed. Typical measures of innovativeness, if by no means the only ones, are time to market, the rate of successful as against failed innovations, and new products' share of total sales. Inward innovation should also be considered under this heading: the continuous renewal of systems and processes, methods and practices, structures and technologies. Decline of innovativeness is a warning sign of the first order.

The third field is productivity or better still *productivities*. In the past, it usually sufficed to measure a *single* productivity, that of work. Today, at least three measurements are needed: the productivity or work, of capital, and of time. And one would be well advised already to consider a fourth, *the productivity of knowledge*, although nobody can yet say how to define it. Productivities are telling only when expressed in terms of added value, i.e. the value added per worker (labor productivity), per invested monetary unit (capital productivity), and per unit of time. Not every company can grow all the time, but every company can constantly improve. To this day, no limit to the improvement of productivity is in sight.

The fourth measure of success is *attractiveness to good people*. Not how many workers join or leave a company – the fluctuation rate – is the key, but which ones. If good people seem to be jumping ship or the company finds it hard to recruit such people, it is time to sit up and pay attention. Good people quitting, regardless at what level, should be a matter for the boss. Although their minds will not usually be changed, such people can tell their superiors the most important and hidden truths – assuming their superiors are willing to hear them.

Liquidity is the fifth measure. It is a time-honored truth that companies can get by for quite a long time without making a profit, but never without liquidity. To increase profit at the expense of liquidity is a dangerous maneuver – for instance by extending payment deadlines in order to increase margins. Companies generally know what to do when their profitability is threatened: they shed bad operations. Constraints on liquidity, on the other hand, usually elicit the wrong response: the best operations are sold, because only they can bring in enough money, and quickly.

Sixth, the company's *profit requirement*, which only rarely can be inferred from the profit as such, indeed not from the financial indicators provided by the accounts department. It emerges from the answer to the question: *What is the minimum profit we need still to be in business tomorrow?* Almost invariably, it turns out that the minimum, thus understood, is distinctly higher than what most people would be prepared to accept as a maximum.

PROFIT

After hundreds of years of the use of the word "profit", first by merchants, then by professors, and latterly by consultants, auditors, and investment bankers, one would imagine that its meaning had been settled beyond all debate. Yet that is not the case. Perhaps better than ever, today we know how to create and manipulate profit forecasts, to interpret statistics selectively, and to deceive the media. Meanwhile, the concept of profit remains poorly understood and is thus often used wrongly and indeed misleadingly.

The more somebody talks about profit, the more skepticism is warranted, until such time as the intended meaning becomes clear. This applies particularly when the talk is of an "optimum" or "maximum" profit.

In leading a business, the idea of a profit maximum is largely useless. What is helpful, by contrast, is the profit minimum. It leads to the question how much the company must *at least* earn to stay in business – not only to service today's obligations, and not just to do business today, but to stay in business. This is a question apart from those accountants are in the habit of asking. For truly professional corporate leadership, I recommend going even a step further and to cease talking about profit altogether.

For there fundamentally is no such thing as profit, there are only costs. First, the costs of doing business today, and second, the costs of staying in business in the future – which may mean going into an entirely new business.

Costs of the first kind are known and can be entered in the books. We do not know the costs of the second kind, we cannot account for them because we have neither receipts nor invoices as proof. Yet they are as real as the costs in the books. If we are not able to pay these costs, the company will have no future. If attention is paid to costs, not profits, major leadership errors become much less likely. Too simplistic a concept of profit, on the other hand, has usually spelled doom for a business.

SHAREHOLDER

Fundamental misconceptions about the nature of economic activity have led to severe confusion. Wall Street's vast promotional machine invented the "investor" and made the world believe that this figure was an entrepreneur, more still, the prototype of the new, modern, especially entrepreneurial entrepreneur. A term once used quite matter-of-factly, or even with the pejorative connotations of the word "speculator," was suddenly elevated to the rank of model and yardstick of entrepreneurial activity.

This misunderstanding and its rapid spread to become the norm of good business is one of the decisive factors in the wrong course that much of the business world has steered since the early 1990s. Though chastened by several crises since, we have not yet broken the spell of this misconception.

An investor is not an entrepreneur

No doubt every entrepreneur is also an investor. But: Is every investor also an entrepreneur? Developments in the stock and financial markets have contributed to blurring, in the eyes of the public, an important distinction, that between the entrepreneur-shareholder and the investor-shareholder. The same piece of paper may vouchsafe ownership of a company and ownership of a share, and the law equally makes no distinction. Yet in economic and societal terms, the difference could not be greater.

If you can't sell, you have to care

A new capitalism has been invented, or so many people believe. Some lament this invention; far more have welcomed it, often euphorically. Yet whatever one's own attitude may be: So far, only half the truth has been noticed, and only that half seemed to matter. Now, gradually, we are having to come to terms with the other half, as has long been the case in Japan. Across the ages, capitalists have been aware of this piece of ancient wisdom: "If you can't sell, you have to care!" Investors play a short game; their interest in their shares lasts only while they pay. Entrepreneurial activity, by contrast, is a long-term undertaking.

The investor-shareholder bails out when difficulties arise – he sells. And if he is smart, he will make his investments in such a way as to make them easily to dispose of if necessary. He can do so by, for instance, sticking to highly liquid markets, where even large holdings can be sold with no difficulty. The entrepreneur-shareholder, when the going gets tough, will respond very differently: She will fight – "she cares." *Why* is not the issue; what matters is that she does. One will fight because she cannot sell. To another, his company represents more than a money-making machine, it is a life's work and often that of generations. A third may struggle because she never again wants to be tethered to a dependent job. They all fight, whatever for. Not because they are heroes, but for want of a choice. The alternative would be to go down with their ships.

Money: the primary resource

Investors are interested primarily in a *single* resource, money, which they seek to maximize. The task of the entrepreneur is by its nature directed at *several* resources; it is defined as a combination of resources that require creative and, as far as possible, productive balancing.

The investor-shareholder is interested only in the financial yield of his investment. He needs not worry about anything else, except perhaps as indicators of what shares to buy. Of course, the investor-entrepreneur is not indifferent to financial yields. She, however, of necessity is interested in the performance and general health of the business as whole, that is to say in all factors relevant to performance, even if this is inconvenient and sometimes a burden. She has no choice in the matter.

Investors depend on the stock market. But for its existence, they could neither pursue nor fulfill their ambitions. They would have to morph into entrepreneurs. Entrepreneurs, on the other hand, are not fundamentally in need of the stock market. Important though it is, entrepreneurs predate stock exchanges by longer even than they predate banks. What is more, they survived even as banks and stock markets collapsed and were closed temporarily. Contrary to widespread belief, the stock market is not just a place where capital is obtained. It is as often a system for the destruction of capital. In more neutral terms, we could call it a system for the evaluation of capital, which should, however, not mislead us as to the accuracy of these valuations.

Especially when they are of the shareholder-value-type, investors occur only in bull markets. Only then can they cultivate the illusion of creating value. In a bear market, the situation is reversed: Investors actively destroy value and capital, because they can make a profit only on the short side. The lower valuations dip, the more investors can profit from short selling and put options. The entrepreneur, by contrast, is a man for all (economic) seasons. He creates value just when prices are at their lowest and no investor is willing to buy.

STAKEHOLDER

The dominant ideas of the 1990s about how to run a business well – above all, the shareholder and shareholder value – have lost their appeal. Gradually, people are coming to suspect that it is precisely these ideas about the leadership, judgment, and valuation of companies based on them that led to one of history's biggest bubbles and all its disastrous consequences. But instead of taking a break to reflect and rethink the whole matter from the ground up, the next hoax, the next error is launched upon the world of business. The stakeholder has replaced the shareholder.

True, the argument goes, a business cannot be run for the benefit of a single group, the shareholders; instead, it is necessary to consider several interested parties, all the stakeholders. Yet several errors, perhaps more dangerous still, are bound up with the concept.

Stakeholder orientation leads to poor management

Historically speaking, the stakeholder approach predates the doctrine of the shareholder. It was formulated in 1952 by Ralph Cordiner, at the time CEO of General Electric, in response to the question to whom the top management of a publicly listed company owed responsibility.

As important and apt as the question was, Cordiner's answer falls short. The stakeholder approach failed, and its failure is the very reason the supposedly better shareholder approach was developed in the first place. Its inventor, Alfred Rappaport, believed it to be the only way to get "lazy" managers to step up.

Low returns were no longer to be justified with reference to the interests of all stakeholders. Rappaport and other correctly recognized that management trying or pretending to consider all interested parties, being everything to everyone, as it were, in fact meant abnegating all responsibility. Whatever the challenge, the excuse of having to consider this or that interest was always open. Whether it was the interests of the workforce and unions, of suppliers, the public, science, or politics – there was always a seemingly compelling reason for bad corporate performance.

The business itself is at the center

The stakeholder approach did not inherently make good leadership impossible. Even in its heyday, some companies were excellently run. General Electric itself is a case in point. However, the stakeholder approach enabled poor management to evade responsibility by recourse to reasons that, on the terms of this approach, seemed entirely plausible and unassailable.

A theory of corporate leadership that places interest groups at its center, however it may define them and how many of them there are, inevitably puts the business at the mercy of shifting balances of power within and between such interest groups. This leaves management without a yardstick by which its performance might reliably be measured. The results are disastrous, as history proves.

There is only one way to provide a business with right and good leadership, and that is to put the business itself at the center. This means that management must act in the interest of the company's performance and competitiveness. What it does not mean is just to look at short-term profits and share prices. We have clear enough standards for long-term, future-oriented top-level management.

What is good for the company may not be equally good for each interested party, but it does enable the largest possible number of legitimate interests to be satisfied. A business that is doing poorly ends up being unable to satisfy any interests.

Securing jobs is not a company's purpose

To argue against shareholder and stakeholder value is not to lapse into welfare statism, as some might suppose. It does not men placing job creation above all else. This should become clear when the company, its performance, and capacity for functioning are placed at the center.

The task of a business is to deliver an economic service to the market, which means: a service to the customer. It meets its obligation to society by creating satisfied customers and, indirectly, markets. If it takes a large workforce to do so, the unions will no doubt be please, but if the company can fulfill its task only by shrinking its workforce, it must not be prevented from doing so. Customer satisfaction is to be placed above job preservation.

Customers are not stakeholders

Defenders of the stakeholder approach will be quick to pounce on this emphasis on the customer and claim that customers, too, are stakeholders. Yet this is a grievous error with respect to the logic of doing business and managing a company. Customers are not an interest group, because they have no interest in the company. However much customers may appreciate a particular supplier, they ultimately are indifferent to the supplying company because, as customers, they have a choice.

In a market economy, having a choice defines the customer as such. If customers are dissatisfied with one company's products or services, they will turn elsewhere. For that reason, it is unrealistic to expect loyalty from customers, though one should of course do everything to secure it. In truth, what looks like loyalty always results from a calculation: Customers pay for the utility they expect to receive.

At this point, the standard objection is that customers have an interest in a company's survival because they are need of and dependent on a supplier. No doubt customers do need suppliers, but in a market economy, at least in a functioning one, there are always several ways to obtain goods and services. What is in the vital interest of customers is *not* to become dependent on a single supplier, which would mean no longer being a customer but, for want of choice, shackled to a monopoly. No matter how close and cordial relations between customer and supplier may be, their foundation remains customers' satisfaction in terms of fulfilling their needs, and having a choice.

There is only one reliable guide to leading a business well: to serve customers better than competitors are able. Customer utility and competitiveness are thus the two measures, neither corruptible nor manipulable, by which management can orient itself.

INFORMATION

We have more data, more information, more communication technology than ever before. Nevertheless – or perhaps for this very reason – top executives regularly list communication as being among their greatest challenges. This becomes less mysterious when we consider terms closely associated with communication – like data, information, and knowledge – in context. Most people will claim "actually" to know perfectly well what these terms mean. That their definitions are long out of date would not be much of a problem if we still lived in a world of "things." But that is no longer the case.

We may now know more about these terms, but clearly not enough really to understand them. And it is quite possible that our understanding may have several more changes to go through. Though we cannot yet hope for a complete picture, some developments are clear enough, and the following insights may help avoid errors and foster effective management.

"Big data" does not equal information, and information does not equal knowledge

Businesses are unlikely to suffer from a lack of data. If anything, having too much is the problem. Information, however, continues to be scarce. Nor can one rely on everybody knowing how to see past mere data and identify relevant information. Big data is a new world of

178

enormous size and variety, of data generated and diffused with unprecedented speed. But data alone – even "big data" – does not tell a story. Data is not the same as information; nor does information equal knowledge. Information emerges from differences and hence distinctions: "Information is a difference that makes a difference," as the cyberneticist Gregory Bateson put it.

All noise, no signal?

Our longstanding chief statistician used to say, "give me a number, and I'll tell you what it means." He was a master of the art of relating bits of data to each other creatively and working out the difference that made a difference. In these days of fake news and alternative facts, it is far from irrelevant what data we correlate with each other. "Data are statements of fact," explained Stafford Beer, the managerial cyberneticist. "Whatever is 'given' is a fact. Fact is that which is the case. The human being cannot normally discover the facts in the data." Conflicting signals end up being perceptible only as noise: "Noise … a meaningless jumble of signals. Counterproductive because it is mistaken for information."

In the same book, Beer adds: "Information is that which CHANGES us. Noise becomes data – when the fact in it is RECOGNIZED. Data become information – when the fact in them is susceptible to action."[10] To extract from the hodgepodge and vast quantity of data any usable information becomes possible only when data can be placed in significant relations with each other.

That this actually happens cannot yet be assumed, even in the most "advanced" companies. It strains belief to see just how often corporate figures are not put into relation, that differences are not expressed in percentages, and that index calculations are simply omitted. The most important items in a budget must always display comparative values and differences, and they must be part of drawing up the budget, not added in a later review stage. What is compared to what depends on individual cases. As a rule, comparisons are made to earlier time periods or figures, other divisions, benchmarks, or other budget items, which is particularly important when structural changes are made as part of the budgeting process.

Numbers and figures are not objective quantities, though they may look like it and are often taken as such. They are in need of interpretation, which often leaves considerable scope. For this reason, every budget must contain structural information – the most important items should be expressed as index figures. They allow a pattern to be extracted from the data, and only from the patterns can we glean any information.

Management is steering, regulating, and guiding – bringing about a change – in complex systems *by means of information and communication*. This can be brought about by interference from outside the system or by influence working within it. In the latter case, we refer to self-steering, self-regulation, and self-guidance.

"... what could have been said"

In connection with management, the term "information" should therefore not be taken in its everyday meaning. The kind of information we are dealing with here refers to the signals, data, and messages that signify differences and in turn trigger further differences or effect changes. In the sense that information makes a difference, a piece of information constitutes a distinction, but above all a decision and a new insight. But even this is not yet sufficient for the nature of information to be understood. To paraphrase W. Ross Ashby, a neuroscientist and, alongside Norbert Wiener, the most important pioneer of cybernetics, information is not what is said, but what is left unsaid, even though it could have been said. Only when I know from what context a message emerges can I know what it means.

KNOWLEDGE MANAGEMENT

Among the most glittering buzzwords in the early days of the New Economy, "knowledge management" is heard rather less often these days. This is not to say that is has become less meaningful since – on the contrary, it is more important than ever. What has declined is the status of the early, somewhat naïve ideas about knowledge management that developed around that time. If one cuts through the mystification and gets to the bottom of the matter, it turns out that what is usually termed knowledge management is in fact something altogether different: data, information, and often simply document management. Of course it helps to develop better-ordered ways of storing information in order to make it more easily accessible to a large number of people – and especially the right people – in more situations. But new and better forms of storing and retrieving information do not yet constitute knowledge management.

Clear evidence for this is provided by the internet, which is not a system of knowledge, though it contains huge mountains of data. Yet for anyone looking for something there, the problem of retrieval not only remains unsolved, but continues to grow in line with the quantity of information available. Until such time as effective new solutions enter the market, as they surely will, the most powerful search engines only serve to exacerbate the problem. What to do with the tens or hundreds of thousands, often millions of search results pre-sorted by algorithms? How to make sense of them? We cannot so much as assess their relevance, less still "know" a fraction of their content in any meaningful sense of the word. To speak of knowledge management in this situation would be premature. As it stands, knowledge is something that has nothing to do with IT, but a lot with brains and more still with reason and intelligence.

If I may be forgiven for being flippant, knowledge is something that is stored between two ears, not transmitted between two IP addresses.

How do people change their knowledge?

It is possible to learn and teach, understand and grasp, transmit and receive, forget and remember. All these activities have something to do with knowledge. The most important part of knowledge management is surely thinking, thinking ahead, and hopefully thinking *right* – in the sense of logical conclusions, which may also include fuzzy logic. All the aforementioned are aspects of dealing with knowledge. To which one might add pondering, contemplating, and realizing; researching, discovering, inventing, and innovating, which, maybe and hopefully, will be done far better than ever.

Of course one could call all this "management," which would be about as useful as referring to cooking as "food management," the performance of a Beethoven symphony as "sound management," or a painting by Monet or Cezanne as "color management."

The whole problem thus needs to be reframed, for knowledge as such cannot, for the time being, be managed. Nobody saw this more clearly than the man who was the first to grasp the importance ok knowledge for modern societies, and who coined the terms "knowledge society" and "knowledge worker." This man was Peter F. Drucker, and he did so not in the context of the New Economy or the euphoria surrounding artificial intelligence, but as early as 1969, in his book *The Age of Discontinuity*.[11]

What can and must be managed is not knowledge, but working with knowledge and the people who do so, the so-called knowledge workers. The distinction between knowledge, knowledge work, and knowledge workers must be borne in mind. Only then can management become effective in this sphere and produce results.

Making knowledge productive

Knowledge – and this is a matter of common agreement – ranks alongside complexity as the most important resource for economic activity today, and more still in the future. This applies equally to all other spheres of society. Complexity and knowledge are already the most valuable resources, even if at present they are hard to quantify and evaluate. Anyone successful in going beyond management merely of data and information will be in possession of a hard-to-match competitive advantage. A key role will be played by the further development of algorithms, and a greater significance still falls to heuristics.

To make knowledge *productive*, however, requires management, management of knowledge work and man-

184

agement of the knowledge worker – the brainworker, if you will. Once that is understood, it will be possible to employ the forms of communication that truly enable the optimum utilization of existing knowledge. This calls not for computers, but for particular arrangements of interpersonal communication, i.e. communication systems, which were first studied at the time modern cybernetics emerged. Its foundations were laid in the famed Macy Conferences (after the Josiah Macy, Jr. Foundation) in the 1940s. Among its most eminent pioneers are Alex Bavelas, Heinz von Foerster, and particularly Stafford Beer.

REORGANIZATION

Few words make managers as nervous as "reorganization." They have every reason to shy away from major
organizational changes, especially when they entail the
dismantling, merging, restructuring, or winding down of
entire departments, manufacturing plants, or corporate
divisions. On the other hand, there are those who pursue
a strategy of permanent reorganization and restructuring
as a way of "keeping things moving." I have little sympathy with this approach. "Organisitis" doesn't just sound
like an unpleasant disease, it is a dangerous error in the
leadership of both businesses and people.

Organizing or functioning?

The difference between creating a new division of labor
and its functioning is illustrated by the following little
story about the reorganization of the game of chess. It ex-
emplifies the interaction between structure and function
of the decision-making processes quite vividly. As we all
know, at either side of the chessboard there sits a player
who plays chess "integrally", i. e. in full awareness of the
rules of the game and able at every moment to obtain a
full picture of the state of play – real-time control in the
best sense of the word .

Somebody is watching the two opponents. He sees the
players' nervousness and tension, and how long it takes
for each to make her move – clearly this game is stressful,

inefficient, and cruel, and thus a prime candidate for reorganization! According to the widely agreed doctrine, organization means grouping equal elements together and putting a capable person in charge. Anything to do with money is grouped under finances, anything to do with people under HR, anything to with computers under IT, anything to do with customers under marketing etc. So what is "equal" in a chess set? All pawns are grouped together and put under the charge of a head pawn. The rooks, too – a small department, admittedly, but an important one, so a rook manager is appointed. And the knights? The organizer hesitates. Their tasks seem to be highly complicated and important – so place them under a single leadership or each one separately? Bearing cost in mind, give them both one boss, and maybe rethink it later. The bishops? Straightforward movements, just one boss. Clearly king and queen are so important that no expense should be spared, so of course each gets a manager, and the CEO himself manages the king.

An admirable solution: less stress, more efficiency – not right away, admittedly, but once everybody has gotten used to the new system and the benefits of specialization are appreciated. Well, management seems a bit unwieldy. So let's appoint a three-person executive board for king, queen, and knights, and four middle managers for the other figures. Given the "business's" complexity, that hardly seems too much. Hence we have an expanded management board of seven people, with the middle managers attending executive meetings as required.

Yet this gives rise to a new problem: coordination! No big deal, after all, tried and pragmatic solutions are available: A board meeting every Monday, usually including middle management, because they provide much-needed information. The pawn leader is the first to present, telling the meeting where his pawns have moved in the previous week and which opposing chessmen have been captured. He knows that the manager of the bishops is angry with him for moving a pawn where he had wanted to move a bishop. The bishop manager presents his situation and puts forward a motion that the head pawn vacate the square by Wednesday in order to allow a bishop to threaten the opposing queen. The head of knights objects vehemently, arguing that with the support of a rook and two pawns, he was position to put the king in check in three moves – emotions begin to run high, the meeting is in disarray.

Refunctioning: self-organization

Instead of rebuilding or reorganizing, consider "refunctioning." To find new forms for existing department to cooperate can lead to a completely new way of functioning. The key to this is self-organization in line with complexity. The self-organization of systems depends on rules that regulate or literally "rule" the behavior of the system's elements – people, in an organization – and govern their interaction. A new function is brought about by new rules.

An example may be found in the replacement of intersections controlled by traffic lights with traffic circles or roundabouts. Though we may have at our disposal the technical means to regulate even the most complicated intersections digitally in order to adapt them to traffic flows, this is only one solution to keep traffic flowing. Replacing many such intersections with a radically simple gyratory solution can achieve the same purpose better, more organically, at a lower cost. This solution follows a different principle: Instead of command signals in the form of stoplights, it relies on the motorists' self-regulation. A traffic circle operates according to two simple and familiar rules. The intelligence required for coordinating thus passes from the computers controlling traffic lights to the drivers themselves, enabling them to self-organize.

An orchestra, too, does not need to be reorganized to play a symphony by Mozart instead of one by Beethoven. What changes is the "software," in this case the sheet music by which the musicians play. The musicians must suddenly alter their control and coordination radically. Yet perfection remains, although no sequence of notes is identical across the two "programs." The precondition is the musicians' rigorous training.

As these examples show, self-organization in practice is a lot less complicated than one might think. And self-organizing abilities require far less philosophical baggage than certain treatises on the matter might suggest. The constants on change are particular rules. Nature has its own set of laws. Organizations function by systems politics – or systems-cybernetic governance – which triggers the quantum leap from regulation to self-regulation, from organization to self-organization.

In businesses, the necessary regulatory instances are the general purposes, values, and rules of functioning.

These regulators are the result of normative decisions. Decisions are normative when they are fundamental, general, and timeless in character. Basic decisions of corporate policy are fundamental – or original – because they cannot be deduced from other sources. They are general in that they apply to all of an organization's parts and activities. They are timeless because they last until they need to be changed – which, in turn, can be done only by fundamental decisions.

DIGITALIZATION

In my experience, about 70 per cent of top executives currently view digitalization as the greatest challenge facing them. Around half of them see considerable opportunity in this development, but in many cases, it is still not clear what they will really consist of, and what direction digitalization will take in various sectors. For the other half, threats seem to predominate for the time being. Around 30 per cent have been long been working on the introduction of digital solutions and see developments to date as vindicating their earlier decisions. The picture gets really interesting, however, when I ask CTOs or heads of IT how they deal with the challenges in technology or their business models, or quite specifically with the implementation of digitalization schemes. What emerges is that it is not so much complicated technology that scuppers these projects – it is the vast complexity that soon exceeds the capacity of conventional project management. Yet digitalization requires its own systems and processes of project management, as able to cope with dynamic complexity as with self-organization and -regulation, the principles of evolution, uncertainty, dynamics, change, and transformation.

Evolving operating systems

Functionally, these management systems are comparable to the operating systems of computers and the nervous systems of organisms. Much as the right functioning of a computer is enabled only by its operating system, a cell by its DNA, and an organism by its nervous system, an organization can function only if it is equipped with the right management system. Right, complexity-adapted, and systems-cybernetic management thus constitutes the *social* and *evolving* "operating system" for organizations and projects of all sizes and kinds.

Digitalization and Systems Cybernetics share a foundation

Many today refer to system-cybernetic management as "completely new" only because they have never seriously studied the matter. But it was developed at the same time as the foundations for today's information technology. Indeed, some of the same pioneers were involved in laying the foundations for computers and the management of organizations, for they recognized early on that both were subject to the same laws. Among these pioneers were the mathematician and founder of modern cybernetics, Norbert Wiener, who in 1948 published his book *Cybernetics: Control and Communication in the Animal and the Machine*. Another was the British neuroscientist Ross W. Ashby, author of two revolutionary works: *Design for a Brain. The Origin of Adaptive Behaviour* (1952) and *An Introduction to Cybernetics* (1956). Also at its cradle stood the likes of Alan Turing, a pioneer of algorithms, Claude Shannon, the creator of information theory, John von Neumann, inventor of the modern computer, Heinz von Foerster, head of the Biological Computer Laboratory, and Gregory Bateson, the path-breaking information theorist. Another crucial figure is Stafford Beer, who recognized that the same rules could be applied to the organization as well as the control and self-regulation of businesses. His book *Cybernetics and Management* (1959) was the first application of Wiener's *Cybernetics* to the management of large organizations. Later, Beer designed the "viable systems" model in analogy the human nervous system as a framework for organizing businesses.

With their early theories about information and communication, algorithms and heuristics, and the design and control of complex systems they created the preconditions both for the actually existing "cyberspace" of today *and* for the cybernetics of managing complex systems. This new, radically innovative cybernetic management was ahead of its time. The mechanistic ideas of management formed in the industrial society were to hold sway for decades yet and be taught at thousands of universities and business schools – and they still are. Yet all it would take to change this is to join together knowledge that has always belonged together.

INTERCONNECTEDNESS

With everybody taking about digitalization, it should be emphasized that what is new is not digital technology itself, but what it enables us to do at its present level of power, speed, and memory. It offers us the opportunity for interconnectedness to a hitherto unimaginable degree – *the connection of everything with everything on a global scale*. With it, the historic coordinating instances of time and space lose their meaning.

Interconnectedness is the driving principle of evolution, of the development of something new that had previously not existed even in rudimentary form. What former methods and means allowed us to do only separately, we can now do together; and what once we could do only consecutively, we now can do simultaneously. The laws of synergy and simultaneity open up new spaces for action and innovation. As natural laws, they may yet turn out to be more important and powerful than gravity.

Interconnection and simultaneity bring about a completely new level of power, higher by orders of magnitude, of processes in terms of speed and effectiveness, intelligence, creativity, and complexity, and to completely new qualitative and quantitative abilities and qualities of systems.

Great as that may sound: Interconnectedness is not enough. For there are two kinds of interconnectedness, right and wrong. Only the right kind of interconnection can produce excellent results. It is one thing to know than an object consists of about 15 kilograms of carbon, 4 kg of nitrogen, 1 kg of calcium, half a kilogram of phosphorus and sulfur, about 200 grams of salt, 150 g of potassium, chloride, and a number of other substances, mixed with quite a lot of water – but what do we know when we know this much? Basically, nothing. Influenced by conventional scientific thinking and its logic, only few will reply, well, it depends how we organize these substances … But that is exactly the point. These raw materials are what we get if we separate a human being into its constituent material elements. What remains if we deprive living being of that which makes them living beings is nothing special. What counts are not the materials. What counts is their organization, the pattern, the order they display, or the information and proper interconnectedness that imparts an order to the material. Life is not matter and energy, life is *informed* matter and energy. What a system consists of is less important than the information that interconnects, orders, and organizes the elements – this is crucial.

School chemistry lessons taught us that from oxygen and hydrogen, something radically new is formed – water. The radically new aspect is that the component elements, the atoms themselves, display none of water's traits. You can't wash in oxygen, and hydrogen won't quench your thirst. Water is formed only by the appropriate interconnection of atoms. Another kind of interconnection produces explosive oxyhydrous gas.

The *right* interconnection of people with each other leads to cooperation and consensus for solutions that can emerge autonomously, to the unfurling of creativity, the utilization of necessary knowledge, the bolstering of intelligence, and the synergy and integration of socio-emotional energy for the effective implementation of these solutions. Wrong interconnection prevents cooperation, and is retarding, blocking, dysfunctional, and often destructive in its effects.

AGILITY

"Agility" has found its way into the lexicon of management only quite recently. Supple, sprightly, dexterous, fleet-footed, quick-witted, swift, and acute – any of these sound familiar? Haven't we been there before? And if not, which of them matter? Some sectors have long had to be agile. Yet there are still sectors that, by the nature of their business, never could and still cannot be agile I the sense described. Their investments are made against a long-term horizon, and they require correspondingly long payback periods. Examples are parts of the insurance business, the energy sector, and the pharmaceutical industry. Relative to their long-term orientation in business, they too have often been flexible, quick, and dexterous, but by the nature of their business not from one day to the next, but within the often decades-long periods within which they framed their business model.

Today, it is information technology in particular that has come under pressure from the huge acceleration in digitalization. Whereas IT, by its function, was once a follower, it is now forced to take on the function of a pioneer. It must lead progress, compete in a race as hotly contested as few have been before, and explore uncharted territory in nearly all its applications. There is no room for cherished old habits or nostalgia.

Stop doing the wrong things!

The time has come systematically to abandon the ways of the past. For we have to assume and prepare for the case that noting of the old will be able to be carried over into the New World. This idea of a *systematic waste disposal* is a huge mental challenge – after all, there is no experience or knowledge to guide us through uncharted territory. Nothing can be prognosticated as such. All we have to work with are scenarios. The methods by which the Old World could innovate and solve problems no longer work, and trying to improve them would only make things worse.

Purposes are even more important than targets

Advanced organizations nowadays are generally quite good at coping effectively with targets. Only few managers, however, also use the technique of defining *purposes* clearly and to set them in place of targets. The devil, as we know, is in the detail. Getting lost in detail can mean losing sight of the bigger picture, the purpose of an innovation. It is a typical experience that, when redesigning organizational processes – particularly in IT – it is of critical importance regularly to ask what *purpose* one is actually out to achieve. Otherwise, one will risk getting bogged down in details that do nothing to further that purpose.

Added to which is the impossibility, in genuinely new situations, of setting plausible targets. When that is the situation, it should nevertheless be possible to state a purpose for any given undertaking. The purpose is the "master control" of implementation.

We shall see if agility, as word in management, has much of a future. The methods needed for mastering the manifold new challenges belong to the class of systems cybernetics. They require knowledge of complexity and how to master it, how to use it to advantage amid the uncertain and unplannable, how not to get tied up in the complications of old rulebooks and long-term ties. Knowledge of how to utilize tight control circuits in real time control systems, in organization hubs with reliable coordination, how to use the evolutionary logic of trial and error correctly, to work in parallel rather than in sequence, and how – beyond algorithms – to work with heuristics. Agility could thus be understood as a quality of systems on their path to viability: the capacity for living and functioning.

SUSTAINABILITY

The terms "sustainable" and "sustainability" came into fashion in management in the late 2000s. They served as a counterweight to the short-term horizon of shareholder value and associated ideas. In this respect, they were an instance of progress, containing as they do the notions of permanence, durability, and continuity. Sustainability is the opposite of a behavior directed at short-term and fast financial gains. It is linked to the idea of using resources carefully. But it also often taken to denote the idea of upholding a state of affairs, a pattern of behavior, a form of doing business, in perpetuity. What this testifies to is often an obsolete concept of stability.

Important though sustainability may be, organizations and most other institutions in society should be capable of more. They must be able to *adapt anew, again and again*, to circumstances and events that nobody foresaw – because they are entirely unforeseeable.

As I have mentioned, the term "stability" is preferred in cybernetics. But what is required is the ability to *bring stable conditions into being again and again*. What is needed are ultra- and polystability going far beyond stability in the conventional sense.

Sustainability is a valuable, progressive step. But it must be followed by the next logical step, which is *viability*. Viability means a system's capacity for maintaining its ability to function indefinitely. A system must be able to cope with a change of resources. This is true also for the substitution of one technology for another, the change from one mode of production to a superior one, from one distribution channel to a newer, richer, and more up-to-date one. It is the capacity for evolution.

NOTES

1 Paul C. Martin/Walter Lüftl, *Der Kapitalismus. Ein System, das funktioniert*, Berlin 1990.

2 Gunnar Heinsohn/Otto Steiger, *Eigentum, Zins und Geld. Ungelöste Rätsel der Wirtschaftswissenschaft*, Reinbek bei Hamburg 2002.

3 As early as the 1970s, the bionics scientist Ingo Rechenberg proved that not only are nature's solutions optimal, but so is the evolutionary path by which they are reached. In philosophy, particularly in epistemology, the most important exponent of evolutionary logic is Karl Popper. See also F. Malik, *Strategy for Managing Complex Systems. A Contribution to Management Cybernetics for Evolutionary Systems*, Campus Verlag, Frankfurt/New York 2016. The book was originally published as *Strategie des Managements komplexer Systeme. Ein Beitrag zur Kybernetik evolutionärer Systeme*, 11th ed., Berne 2015 (1984). The book is the result of a two-year research project supported by the Swiss National Science Foundation. Its manuscript was submitted to the university of St. Gallen as a second dissertation (*Habilitationsschrift*) in 1978.

4 On this, see Viktor Frankl's numerous books; the selected essays in *The Unheard Cry for Meaning: Psychotherapy and Humanism*, New York, 2011, offer a good introduction.

5 Among the most interesting work in this field are the studies by Dietrich Dörner and his collaborators, for instance the Tanaland and Lohhausen experiments. For an overview, see Diet-

rich Dörner, *Die Logik des Misslingens. Strategisches Denken in komplexen Situationen*, Reinbek bei Hamburg 2003.

6 See Friedrich August von Hayek, *Law, Legislation and Liberty*, vol. 3, London 1979, pp. 155 ff.

7 See e.g. John Eccles, *Evolution Of The Brain: Creation Of The Self*, London 1989.

8 See Michael E. Porter, *Competitive Advantage*, New York 1985.

9 Notable studies of this phenomenon include those by Nikolaj Kondratieff, Joseph Schumpeter, Karl Polanyi, Peter F. Drucker, Gerhard Mensch and Cesare Marchetti, R. N. Elliott, and Robert Prechter (see Bibliography).

10 Stafford Beer, *The Heart of Enterprise*, Chichester/New York 1979, pp. 282 f.

11 See Peter F. Drucker, *The Age of Discontinuity. Guidelines to Our Changing Society*, London 1969.

BIBLIOGRAPHY

Ashby, Ross W.: *Design for a Brain*, London 1952.

Bateson, Gregory: *Steps to an Ecology of Mind*, New York 1972.

Beer, Stafford: *Cybernetics and Management*, New York 1959.

Beer, Stafford: *The Heart of Enterprise*, Chichester/New York 1979.

Beer, Stafford: *Brain of the Firm*, New York 1972.

Bresch, Carsten: *Zwischenstufe Leben – Evolution ohne Ziel?*, Munich 1977.

Dörner, Dietrich: *Die Logik des Misslingens*. 5th ed. Reinbek bei Hamburg 2003.

Drucker, Peter F.: *Managing for Results*, London 1964.

Drucker, Peter F.: *The Age of Discontinuity*, London 1969.

Drucker, Peter F.: *The New Realities*, London 1989.

Eccles, John: *Evolution Of The Brain: Creation Of The Self*, London 1989.

Frankl, Viktor: *The Unheard Cry for Meaning: Psychotherapy and Humanism*, New York 2011.

Hayek, Friedrich A.: *Law, Legislation and Liberty*, vol. 3, London 1973–1979.

Heinsohn, Gunnar: *Privateigentum, Patriarchat, Geldwirtschaft*, Frankfurt/Main 1984.

Heinsohn, Gunnar/Steiger, Otto: *Eigentum, Zins und Geld*, Marburg 1996.

Kondratieff, Nikolai D.: *Die langen Wellen der Konjunktur*, in: *Archiv für Sozialwissenschaft und Sozialpolitik*, vol. 56 (1926), pp. 573–609.

Marchetti, Cesare: "Fifty-Year Pulsations in Human Affairs," in: *Futures* 17(3), pp. 376–388.

Marchetti, Cesare: *Society as a Learning System*, in: *Technological Forecasting and Social Change*, vol. 18 (1980).

Martin, Paul C./Lüftl, Walter: *Der Kapitalismus. Ein System, das funktioniert*, Berlin 1990.

Mensch, Gerhard: *Das technologische Patt*, Frankfurt/Main 1975.

Pask, Gordon: *An Approach to Cybernetics*, London 1961.

Pelzmann, Linda: *Triumph der Massenpsychologie*, in: *Malik on Management-Letter*, 11/2002.

Polanyi, Karl: *The Great Transformation*, New York 1944.

Popper, Karl R.: *A World of Propensities*, London 1997.

Porter, Michael E.: *Competitive Advantage*, New York 1985.

Prechter, Robert R. Jr.: *Socionomics*, Gainesville, FL 2003.

Riedl, Rupert: *Strukturen der Komplexität.*, Berlin/Heidelberg 2000.

Riedl, Rupert: *Verlust der Morphologie*, Vienna 2006.

Schumpeter, Joseph A.: *Business Cycles*, New York/London 1939.

Schumpeter, Joseph A.: *Capitalism, Socialism and Democracy*, London 1950.

Tversky, Amos/Kahnemann, Daniel (eds.): *Choices, Values, and Frames*, Cambridge, MA 2000.

Vester, Frederic: *The art of interconnected thinking: ideas and tools for a new approach to tackling complexity*, Munich 2012.

Watzlawick, Paul/Beavin, Janet H./Jackson, Don D.: *Menschliche Kommunikation*, Berne/Stuttgart/Vienna 1974.

Wiener, Norbert: *Cybernetics: Or Control and Communication in the Animal and the Machine*, Cambridge, MA 1948.

SELECTED BOOKS
BY FREDMUND MALIK

Managing, Performing, Living: Effective Management for a New World. Campus Verlag, 2006, 2015.

Navigating into the Unknown. A New Way for Management, Governance and Leadership. Campus Verlag, 2016.

Maucher und Malik on Management: Maxims of Corporate Management. Campus Verlag, 2013.

Strategy for Managing Complex Systems: A Contribution to Managerial Cybernetics for Evolutionary Systems. Campus Verlag, 2016. Based on the 10th edition (2008) of the German original.

Uncluttered Management Thinking: 46 Concepts for Masterful Management. Campus Verlag, 2011.

Bionics – Fascination of Nature. Malik Management Center St. Gallen, MCB-Publishing House, 2007.

Series: "Management: Mastering Complexity":

Volume 1: *Management: the Essence of the Craft.* Campus Verlag, 2010.

Volume 2: *Corporate Policy and Covernance: How Organizations Self-Organize.* Campus Verlag, 2011.

Volume 3: *Strategy: Navigating the Compexity of the New World.* Campus Verlag, 2013.

The Right Corporate Governance: Effective Top Management for Mastering Complexity. Campus Verlag, 2012.